Better Homes and Ga...

SCRAPBOOKING
WITH RECIPES

Ideas for Preserving Kitchen Memories

Better Homes and Gardens® Books
Des Moines, Iowa

SCRAPBOOKING WITH RECIPES

BETTER HOMES AND GARDENS® BOOKS
AN IMPRINT OF MEREDITH® BOOKS

Editor: Carol Field Dahlstrom
Writer: Susan M. Banker
Designer: Angie Haupert Hoogensen
Copy Chief: Terri Fredrickson
Copy and Production Editor:
    Victoria Forlini
Editorial Operations Manager:
    Karen Schirm
Managers, Book Production: Pam
    Kvitne, Marjorie J. Schenkelberg,
    Rick von Holdt
Contributing Copy Editor:
    Margaret Smith
Contributing Proofreaders: Karen
    Grossman, Sara Henderson,
    Karen Schmidt
Photographers: Scott Little, Andy
    Lyons Cameraworks
Technical Illustrator: Chris Neubauer
    Graphics, Inc.
Electronic Production Coordinator:
    Paula Forest
Editorial and Design Assistants:
    Kaye Chabot, Mary Lee Gavin,
    Karen McFadden

MEREDITH® BOOKS
Editor in Chief: Linda Raglan
    Cunningham
Design Director: Matt Strelecki
Executive Editor, Food and Crafts:
    Jennifer Dorland Darling

Publisher: James D. Blume
Executive Director, Marketing:
    Jeffrey Myers
Executive Director, New Business
    Development: Todd M. Davis
Executive Director, Sales: Ken Zagor
Director, Operations: George A. Susral
Director, Production:
    Douglas M. Johnston
Business Director: Jim Leonard

Vice President and General
    Manager: Douglas J. Guendel

Better Homes and Gardens® Magazine
Editor in Chief: Karol DeWulf Nickell

MEREDITH PUBLISHING GROUP
President, Publishing Group:
    Stephen M. Lacy
Vice President–Publishing Director:
    Bob Mate

MEREDITH CORPORATION
Chairman and Chief Executive
    Officer: William T. Kerr

In Memoriam: E. T. Meredith III
    (1933–2003)

All of us at Better Homes and
Gardens® Books are dedicated to
providing you with information and
ideas to create beautiful and useful
projects. We welcome your comments
and suggestions. Write to us at:
Better Homes and Gardens Books,
Crafts Editorial Department,
1716 Locust Street—LN112,
Des Moines, IA 50309-3023.

If you would like to purchase any of
our crafts, cooking, gardening, home
improvement, or home decorating and
design books, check wherever quality
books are sold. Or visit us at:
bhgbooks.com

COVER PHOTOGRAPH: Andy Lyons
    Cameraworks

RECIPES, RECIPES, RECIPES!

We all have them. Boxes brimming with tattered cards, a plastic bag in the bottom drawer filled with favorites, an old cookbook with irreplaceable loose papers wedged inside—yes, we all have those precious recipes tucked away just waiting to be put in some sort of order. Now we have just the solution: Put those treasures into scrapbook pages designed with recipes in mind! What better way to create a family keepsake than to combine photos and priceless recipes?

Many of our fondest memories are those of cooking, eating, or gathering together. Perhaps you have a favorite grandmother's recipe that you want to showcase, or the birthday cake from your teenager's 16th birthday. A trip to Europe may have included a special dish that should be noted, or maybe your little one made cookies for the first time and you have the perfect photo of that special day. Combining photos and recipes is a natural way to preserve those special times in the kitchen.

So grab your scrapbooking supplies and gather the recipes (from boxes, bags, and drawers!) and use your talents to make a cherished scrapbook filled with memories from the kitchen.

Carol Field Dahlstrom

CONTENTS

THE MAKING OF A KITCHEN SCRAPBOOK

CELEBRATING THE HUB OF THE HOUSE

Whether there's one cook at the stove or a party is being hosted, the events that take place in the kitchen deserve to be preserved in creative scrapbook pages.

Kitchens are where favorite dishes are made and savored. It's where families share a love of cooking. Traditions are handed down to the next generation in the kitchen. It's where good conversations blossom. The kitchen is where kids can learn, contribute, have fun, make a mess, and eat and share their creations.

Yes, the kitchen *is* the hub of the house, and this book is devoted to helping you make wonderful and interesting scrapbook pages—all dedicated to the cooks, recipes, and celebrations that hold endearing memories.

To get your ideas flowing, here is a list of events and situations to focus on for pages or entire books devoted to kitchen scrapbooking:

- *Birthday parties*
- *Family reunions*
- *Picnics*
- *Anniversaries*
- *Weddings and bridal showers*
- *Baby showers*
- *Travels*
- *Housewarmings*
- *Holidays*
- *Favorite recipes*
- *Secret family recipes*
- *Toddlers' first meals*
- *Generations in the kitchen*
- *Cookie making*
- *Parties*
- *Potlucks*
- *Neighborhood gatherings*

Once you start, you'll have oodles of ideas for capturing meaningful moments. So roll up your sleeves and get ready to invent spectacular scrapbook pages.

GATHERING THE BASICS

To make the best use of your scrapbooking time, gather these supplies and keep them together:

- *Album and page protectors*
- *Card stock and scrapbook papers (white and colors)*
- *Adhesive*
- *Black pens (such as Zig thin and thick tips)*
- *Straight-edge scissors*
- *Paper cutter*
- *Container for organizing photos and negatives*
- *Storage boxes or bags for supplies*

In addition, you may want to invest in these supplies to add decorative touches:

- *Decorative-edge scissors*
- *Paper punches*
- *Precut paper mats*
- *Stickers and die cuts*
- *Templates*

Before you head to the scrapbooking store, write a list of the pages you plan to make.

With aisle after aisle of wonderfully tempting supplies, your list will help you focus and select the most useful items. (Although, if you see an item too nifty to pass up…don't!)

RECORDING THE RECIPES

Who can deny that much of our lives revolves around food? Creating scrapbook pages with this theme is a wonderful way to organize and collect favorite recipes. As you search for family recipes, not all of them may be in books or on recipe cards. Recipes from days past may be written on scraps of paper, envelopes, or other things. Original drafts will give a scrapbook personality.

Most likely you'll discover recipes recorded in a variety of ways. Some cooks carefully list the ingredients in the order they are used. Some recipes include the method; others simply list the ingredients. You'll find old recipes fascinating as you read such ingredients as "a peck of apples" or "a pint of milk."

If you wish to keep the original recipes intact and not put them in your scrapbook, follow these ideas for copying:

- *Photocopy original recipes in color to maintain originality.*
- *Type recipes on a computer and print them on card stock, vellum, or theme papers.*
- *Handwrite recipes or ask the originator of the recipe to*

ALUMINUM SHERBETS, CIRCA 1950

CHOPPER, CIRCA 1890

write it. For an aged look, choose an appropriate paper to write on or chalk the background and edges.

Here are some other ideas to embellish your recipes:
- *Place a sticker on a recipe card, then add handwriting.*
- *Carefully burn the edges of a printed recipe.*
- *Add a computer-generated, drawn, or sticker border.*
- *Record the recipe on a fairly plain note card.*
- *Computer-generate the recipe.*
- *Write the recipe on a die cut that relates to the subject.*
- *Use a color-coordinated marking pen.*
- *Mount the recipe on scrapbook paper to frame it.*
- *Use photo corners to adhere a recipe card on a page.*

CREATING KEEPSAKE KITCHEN PAGES

As with any scrapbooking, you can make simple or elaborate pages. The huge variety of scrapbooking materials available will make it easy to carry out themes. From stickers to die cuts, rubber stamps to papers, thousands of possibilities await your creativity.

To add a vintage touch to your kitchen scrapbook pages, consider photocopying these antique items:
- *Table linens*
- *Kitchen tools*

- *Cooking-related ads*
- *Aprons, hot pads, and towels*
- *Small appliances*
- *Cookie cutters*
- *Dinnerware*
- *Tableware*

When photocopying and scanning items for personal use in your scrapbooks, be respectful of the copyright interests of others. Look for a © copyright symbol. If you have questions as to whether or not the work is in the public domain, carefully investigate.

Additionally, use the following items to personalize recipe scrapbook pages in a jiffy:
- *Party invitations*
- *Decorative paper napkins*
- *Paper doilies*
- *Business cards*
- *Letters*
- *Awards*
- *Certificates*
- *Restaurant menus*
- *Matchbook covers*
- *Newspaper clippings*
- *Magazine articles*
- *Diary entries*
- *Food wrappers and labels*
- *Nature items, such as leaves*

MAKING YOUR MEMORIES LAST...AND LAST

When selecting items to place on a scrapbook page, determine whether you want your book to be acid-free. If this is a concern, choose such archival supplies as acid-free

and lignin-free paper, acid-free or pH-neutral adhesives, and permanent, fade-resistant inks and pens. If needed, consult the glossary, *pages 6–7.*

Adhesives to secure paper and elements to album pages come in many forms, including photo tape, photo corners, double-sided adhesive dots, squares or strips, glue pens, glue sticks, nonpermanent glue, and bottled glue. Like the materials used for your album, the adhesives can be acid-free. You may wish to keep several types of adhesives on hand, because certain adhesives work better for certain applications.

CHOOSING KEEPSAKE PHOTOS

Preserve precious memories for future generations by including photos that honor people, places, pets, and noteworthy events that evoke kitchen memories. The first rule in sorting through photos is to part with poor exposures. Set aside those that are too dark, too light, out of focus, or meaningless; use only the best photos for your scrapbook pages.

Sort photographs to relate to one another or to an album theme. Although you can affix original photos in your album, if you want to save them for other purposes, photocopy the originals on a color photocopier.

If you have a collection of slides or reel-to-reel 8mm

films, these can be converted to photographs at relatively low cost at photography supply shops or photo studios.

Identify as many people in your photos as you can, and add specific places and dates whenever possible. Ask family members for help, and take your photos to family reunions and get-togethers for help in identification.

Before handling old photos, wash your hands. Dirt and oils from skin are damaging to photos and photo negatives.

Photos that have yellowed, become brittle, or been affixed with tape should be moved to a safer environment. However, you may want to copy the photos before moving them or have them professionally photographed in their current site.

Determine whether to use your heirloom photos in your album or make color photocopies of them. To capture all the shading of black-and-white or sepia-tone photos, make color photocopies of them rather than making black-and-white photocopies. If you decide to use the original photos, consider securing them to the scrapbook pages with photo corners rather than permanently adhering them.

SCRAPBOOKING GLOSSARY

Become familiar with these scrapbooking terms to remember as you shop for materials and start creating pages:

ACID-FREE

Acid is used in paper manufacturing to break apart the wood fibers and the lignin that holds them together. If acid remains in the materials used for photo albums, the acid can react chemically with photographs and cause deterioration. Acid-free products have a pH factor of 7.0 to 8.5. It's imperative that all materials (glue, pens, paper, etc.) used in memory albums or scrapbooks be acid-free.

ACID MIGRATION

Acid migration is the transfer of acidity from one item to another through physical contact or acidic vapors. If a newspaper clipping is put into an album, the area it touches will eventually turn yellow or brown. A deacidification pH factor spray can be used on acidic papers, or the papers can be photocopied to acid-free papers.

ADHESIVE

Scrapbooking adhesives include glue sticks, double-stick tape, spray adhesive, thick white crafts glue, mounting tabs, and other products. Read labels to determine the best adhesive for the intended use.

ARCHIVAL QUALITY

This term is used to indicate materials that have been analyzed to determine that acidic and buffered content is within safe levels for use on scrapbook pages.

BORDERS

Precut strips of patterned or solid paper are used to accent or border scrapbook pages.

BUFFERED PAPER

During manufacture a buffering agent, such as calcium carbonate or magnesium bicarbonate, can be added to paper to neutralize acid contaminant. Such papers have a pH of 8.5.

CARD STOCK

Often used for the base or background, card stock is heavy and has a smooth surface.

CORNER ROUNDER

Used like a paper punch, this tool rounds the corners of photographs and papers.

CRAFTS KNIFE

Commonly known as an X-Acto knife, this tool has a small, sharp blade for cutting paper and other materials.

CROPPING

This term refers to trimming photos to keep only the most important parts of images.

DECORATIVE-EDGE SCISSORS

Available in a wide assortment of cutting blades, these scissors cut paper and other thin materials with wavy, scalloped, or other decorative edges.

DIE CUT
These premade paper shapes are available at most scrapbook and crafts stores and come in many shapes, sizes, and colors. For a fee, some stores will let you use their die-cutting machine with your own paper to create shapes that perfectly coordinate with your layout.

GLOSSY
A smooth, shiny appearance or finish, often used to describe paper, is referred to as glossy.

GLUE STICK
A glue stick is a solid stick-type glue that is applied by rubbing.

JOURNALING
This term refers to text written on scrapbook pages that provides details about the photographs. Journaling can be computer generated, handwritten, or done with adhesive letters, rub-ons, or stencils.

LIGNIN-FREE
Naturally present in most papers, lignin causes paper to yellow when it's exposed to ultraviolet light.

MAT
Varying weights of paper used to frame photographs and memorabilia in layers.

MATTE
A dull surface or finish, not shiny or glossy, is considered matte.

OPAQUE
Opaque colors are dense and cannot be seen through.

PAPER CUTTER
A paper cutter is a tool with a surface for holding the paper and a sharp blade that cuts the paper in a straight line.

PAPER PUNCH
Available in many different shapes, this handheld tool punches out circles, hearts, diamonds, and other shapes in stencil form.

pH FACTOR
The pH factor refers to the acidity of a paper. The pH scale, a standard for measurement of acidity and alkalinity, runs from 0 to 14, each number representing a tenfold increase; neutral is 7. Acid-free products have a pH factor of 7 to 8.5. Special pH tester pens are available to determine the acidity or alkalinity of products.

PHOTO-SAFE
This term is similar to archival quality but is more specific to materials used with photographs. Acid-free is the determining factor for products to be labeled photo-safe.

PROTECTIVE SLEEVES
Plastic to slip over a finished album page, sleeves are side loading or top loading and fit 8½×11- or 12-inch-square pages. Choose only acid-free sleeves. Polypropylene (vinyl), commonly available for office

use, is not archival quality and should not be included in albums.

RUBBER STAMPING
Designs are etched into a rubber mat that is applied to a wooden block. This rubber design is stamped onto an ink pad to transfer the design to paper or other surfaces.

SCRAPBOOKING PAPERS
Scrapbooking papers are usually 12 inches square or 8½×11 inches and include solids, patterns, textures, and vellum.

SEPIA
This is a brown tone, usually associated with photographs that has a warm, antique look.

STENCIL
Made from heavy paper or plastic, a stencil is laid flat on a surface. Paint or another medium is applied through the design openings to transfer the pattern or design.

STICKERS
Available in plastic, paper, fabric, and other materials, stickers can be peeled from backing paper and pressed in place.

TRACING PAPER
This is a transparent paper that is used to trace patterns.

VELLUM
Available in white, colors, and patterns, this translucent paper has a frosted appearance.

GENERATIONS OF RECIPES

Honor favorite family recipes along with the stories that accompany them in keepsake scrapbook pages. Whether recording Grandma's very best desserts or recalling a birthday cake from years past, this delightful chapter will help you preserve those special recipes to pass on from generation to generation.

FAMILY TRADITIONS

A single photograph can capture a moment in time. For a treasured scrapbook page, combine an around-the-table shot like this one with the recipes from the dishes that were served.

WHAT YOU NEED

Recipes
Photo
Two 12-inch squares of
  print background paper
Dark solid paper to complement
  background paper
Antique-looking parchment paper
Metal photo corners

Metal dots, such as The Stamp
  Doctor
Kitchen-theme stickers
Black marking pen
Paper cutter
Computer and printer
Adhesive

WHAT TO DO

1 Computer-generate the headline and journal block. Crop around copy.

2 Adhere stickers to paper; crop. Frame each element with dark paper, and cut dark paper triangles to mount

METAL CORNERS AND DOTS
ADD DIMENSION.

MOUNT CORNER TRIANGLES
ON STICKER SQUARES
FOR INTEREST.

CALL ATTENTION TO A PHOTO
BY DOUBLE-MOUNTING IT.

Family Traditions

A lot of family traditions are recipes that are handed down from generation to generation Great-Grandma Grant & Grandma Johnson are serving the noon meal to Great-Grandpa and the other men that were there to harvest the corn. Great-Grandma was a very good cook The meal would usually consist of pot roast, mashed potatoes & gravy, green beans from the garden, cranberry salad, rye bread from Aunt Julia, and always pie

HEADLINE IDEAS

1. *Dinner at the Farm*
2. *A Feast for the Farmhands*
3. *Gather Round the Table*
4. *Dinner Break*
5. *In From the Fields*
6. *Dinnertime*
7. *Real Comfort Food!*
8. *Grandpa and Guests*

ICE CREAM
SCOOP,
CIRCA 1900

smaller paper pieces, as shown on the apron and rolling pin square. To emphasize the photo, double-mount it with dark and parchment papers.

3 Use a black marking pen to randomly draw scrolls

and lines around the headline and journal boxes. Adhere metal corners to the headline and metal dots to the corners of the journal box.

4 Adhere all pieces in place.

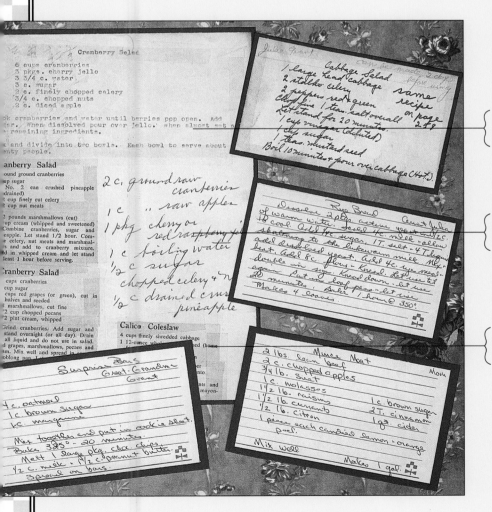

PHOTOCOPY RECIPES ON ANTIQUE-LOOKING PARCHMENT PAPER FOR AN AGED EFFECT.

INCLUDE COPIES OF ORIGINAL HANDWRITTEN AND TYPED RECIPES.

LEAVE ORIGINAL TAPE MARKS TO MAINTAIN AN AGED LOOK.

PUMPKIN PIE

To complete a page or two using very few supplies, create a striking composition similar to this one.

WHAT YOU NEED

Recipe; photos
8½×11-inch green card stock
Card stock in off-white and dark green
Stickers, ivy and kitchen themes
Fine-line marking pens, dark green and black
Paper cutter
Computer and printer; ruler
Adhesive

WHAT TO DO

1 To maintain an aged patina, photocopy the baker's handwritten notes and/or recipe on off-white paper. If you need to reproduce the recipe, handwrite it in black on off-white paper.

PHOTOCOPY ORIGINAL NOTES TO INCLUDE IN LAYOUT. }

USE PAPER THAT CONTRASTS WITH THE BACKGROUND TO FRAME SHAPES. }

COMPUTER-GENERATE A HEADLINE USING A FAINT DROP SHADOW. }

3 eggs
sugar
= 1 C

Pumpkin
Pie

Everyone agrees that my mom's Pum
Pie is the best anywhere. In typica
Mom's recipe (left) is a bit sketchy
this case she only wrote down the ingre
She can't remember. Several years ag
managed to obtain the entire recipe
her because it is so very good and
not fathom i- b
written on a scr
paper taped to
inside lid of he
recipe box fore

Pumpkin Pie   Mom

3 eggs, slightly beaten
1 rounded C sugar   } Mix together,
1 can pumpkin (16 oz)   } then add:
½ t pumpkin pie spice
½ + t cinnamon
1½ C milk
Stir together; pour in pie shell (unbaked) - 9"
Bake 15 min. @ 425°; reduce heat to 400° for
45 min. Pie is done when knife comes out clean *

Pumpkin Pie
using Better Homes & Gardens pie crust recipe

HEADLINE IDEAS

1. *Let's Make Pie*
2. *Making Grandma's Pie Recipe*
3. *The Best Pie in the World*
4. *Learning to Make Pie*
5. *The "Pies" Have It*
6. *My Very Favorite Pumpkin Pie*

SPICE TIN, CIRCA 1930

2 Computer-generate a headline in green tones.

3 Mount the note, recipe, headline, and photos on dark green card stock. Trim a ⅛-inch border around each piece. Apply kitchen stickers to dark green paper squares.

4 Arrange and glue the components to the background card stock. Apply ivy stickers to the outer corners of the spread.

5 Journal neatly in dark green around the layout elements.

At my parents' house in Runnells, Bailey is frequently exposed to the old-fashioned ways of doing things, including mowing with an antique mower, using an old iron, and making pies from scratch. Here, she is making Mom's famous pumpkin pie recipe.

Bailey, age 5, March '98

RECORD MEMORIES OF RECIPES IN OPEN AREAS OF DESIGN.

PLACE STICKERS ON PAPER SQUARES FOR DECORATIVE DETAIL.

APPLY STICKERS ON CORNERS TO FRAME THE SPREAD.

GRANDMA'S FAMOUS OATMEAL COOKIES

Record baking secrets to preserve favorite recipes for generations to come.

WHAT YOU NEED

Recipes
Photos
Two 12-inch squares of brown
  card stock
Card stock in gold, dark peach,
  and light peach
8½×11-inch translucent vellum
Buttons
Jute or twine
Dimensional kitchen-theme
  stickers, such as Jolee's
Alphabet punches
Alphabet stamps
Brown ink
Swirl paper clips
Paper cutter
Computer and printer
Adhesive

WHAT TO DO

1 For this design, record the recipes in two ways. Make a photocopy of an original handwritten recipe and reproduce one on a computer using an easy-to-read script font.

COMPUTER-GENERATE A
HEADLINE ON VELLUM.

TIE A BUTTON WITH JUTE
AND GLUE IN PLACE FOR A
SEWN-ON APPEARANCE.

MOUNT A PHOTO ON
COORDINATING COLORS OF
CARD STOCK FOR EMPHASIS.

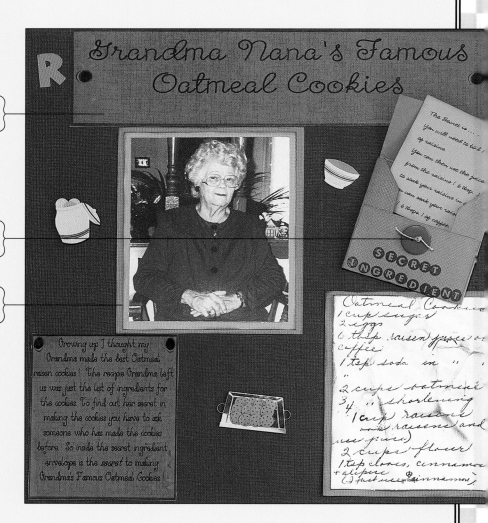

SCOOP, CIRCA 1900

2 To make the headlines and journal blocks, create them on a computer, outlining the copy blocks and adding tack-head embellishments for interest. Print the copy on vellum.

3 Mount recipes on a single piece of card stock and the photos on two coordinating pieces. To give the design a vintage appearance, shade the edges of the card stock with brown ink.

4 Fold small card stock envelope pockets to hold the secret for each recipe. Stamp SECRET INGREDIENT on the pockets and trim them with jute-tied buttons.

5 After the sections are adhered in place, press on kitchen-theme stickers to balance the arrangement.

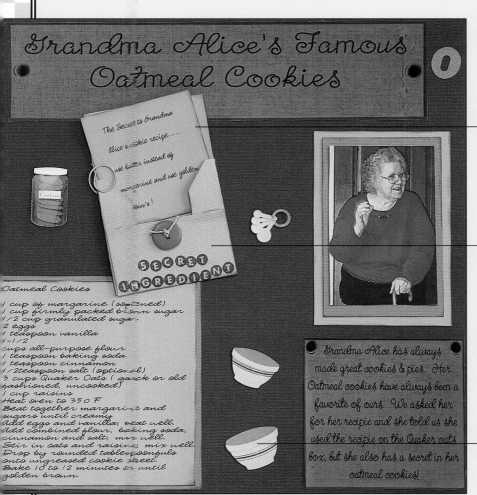

INK PAPER EDGES TO AGE THE PIECES.

FOLD A SMALL POCKET FROM CARD STOCK.

KITCHEN-THEME STICKERS ADD TO THE VINTAGE APPEAL.

MOM'S PEACH PIE!

Whether you boast about pie crust or the whole pie, this clever layout has all the right ingredients.

WHAT YOU NEED

Recipe

Photos

8½×11-inch photocopies of primary-color kitchen fabric and red gingham fabric, plus a small rolling pin

Enlarged copy of kitchen fabric

Card stock in blue and white

Sheer wide white lace

½-inch white alphabet stickers

Paper cutter; scissors

Edging tool; computer and printer

Adhesive

WHAT TO DO

1 To coordinate the background paper with the photograph, this layout uses a photocopy of the curtains hanging to the left of the person in the photo. Create your own background paper in this fashion, choosing a tablecloth, fabric napkin, curtain, towel, hot pad, or other fabric item from your kitchen. Make an enlargement of a detail, such as the canning jars. Photocopy gingham fabric for accent paper and a small rolling pin for the headline.

2 Cut strips from the gingham-print paper, trimming one strip with a scalloped edge. Glue to the top and bottom of the background paper. Glue lace across top edge.

3 Crop the photo as desired, using an edging tool on the corners. Mount the photo to a solid piece of contrasting paper. Trim the solid paper just beyond the photo, using the edging tool on the corners. Mount to a second paper and trim the corners.

4 Silhouette the photographed food. Print the recipe on a computer, adding a colorful border.

5 Adhere the pieces in place. Use sticker lettering to apply a headline to the rolling pin paper.

USE AN EDGING TOOL TO MAKE ORNATE PHOTO CORNERS.

SILHOUETTE PHOTO OF PIE AND HIGHLIGHT THE RECIPE.

COMPUTER-GENERATE THE RECIPE, ADDING A COLORFUL BORDER.

Plain Pastry Crust

1 1/2 c. sifted all purpose flour   1/2 tsp. salt
1/2 c. shortening   4 - 5 tbsp. cold water

Sift flour and salt together; cut in shortening with pastry blender till pieces are the size of small peas. Gently Sprinkle 1 tbsp. water over part of mixture. Gently toss with a fork; push to side of bowl; repeat till all is moistened. Form into ball. Flatten on lightly floured surface. Roll to 1/8" thick.

DAD'S FISHIN' HOLE

After a day with rod and reel, this fisherman serves the catch of the day with his signature Foiled Potatoes.

ROUND THE PHOTO AND MAT CORNERS FOR A POLISHED LOOK.

WOOD-GRAIN PAPER HAS AN AUTHENTIC LOOK.

USE AN EMBELLISHMENT AS A TIE TACK.

COVER CARDBOARD SHAPES WITH FABRIC OR PAPER TO CREATE A TIE.

DIMENSIONAL EMBELLISHMENTS CARRY OUT THE THEME.

WHAT YOU NEED

Recipe; photos
12-inch background paper in
*   natural tones*
Papers in wood grain and dark
*   red plaid; tan card stock*
Tracing paper
Lightweight cardboard
Green plaid fabric or paper
Fish-theme embellishments
Brown alphabet stickers
Pencil; scissors
Paper cutter; corner rounder
Brown marking pen; adhesive

WHAT TO DO

1 Crop the photos as desired, using a corner rounder. Mount photos on tan card stock. Trim card stock ⅛ inch beyond the photo edges. Adhere photos to background.

2 Use a marking pen to write the recipe on a small piece of wood-grain paper, allowing space at the top for the sticker headline. Adhere to red plaid paper, press on headline, and trim border ⅛ inch beyond recipe.

3 To make the signpost, cut a ½×2½-inch piece from wood-grain paper. Mount to red plaid. Trim, leaving a narrow red border around the post. Adhere to the center back of the recipe.

Adhere the sign to the lower right-hand corner.

4 To make tie, trace the patterns, *page 104,* on cardboard; cut out. Trace around patterns on fabric and cut out shapes ¼ inch larger. Fold fabric around cardboard and glue edges to back. For a collar, cut a 10×2½-inch piece of fabric. Fold into a tube; finger-press. Using the photo as a guide, glue the tie pieces to the page.

5 Adhere embellishments to the page and add a fish tie tack.

GRANNY'S SECRETS

Resembling a vintage kitchen apron, this hand-stitched page includes a handy pocket to hold treasured recipe cards.

WHAT YOU NEED

*Recipes on cards; two 12-inch squares of white card stock
14-inch-square of gingham fabric
6×8-inch piece of gingham fabric
Embroidery floss in 3 colors to coordinate with fabric; needle
2 colors of rickrack; letter stickers
Sewing machine and thread
Tracing paper; pencil; scissors
Adhesive*

WHAT TO DO

1 Using three plies of floss, cross-stitch a row of Xs 2 inches from the lower edge of the gingham square, skipping every other square. Machine-stitch two rows of rickrack below the cross-stitches.

2 Center the stitched piece over the background card stock square. Fold the fabric around the card stock edges and crease. Machine-stitch around the edges.

3 For a pocket, cross-stitch three rows across the top of the gingham rectangle, skipping every other square as shown, *below left*.

4 Enlarge and trace the pocket pattern, *page 105.* Cut out the shape. Trace around the shape on card stock; cut out. Center the paper pocket shape on the wrong side of the stitched gingham piece. Fold the fabric around the paper and crease. Machine-stitch rickrack across the top.

5 Place the pocket on the background and stitch in place, adding rickrack around the pocket sides and bottom.

6 Press lettering on white card stock for headline. Adhere headline and recipes. Place additional recipe cards in the pocket.

LEAVE POCKET OPEN AT TOP TO STORE RECIPE CARDS.

CROSS-STITCH GINGHAM FABRIC FOR VINTAGE APPEAL.

MACHINE-STITCH POCKET TO FABRIC-COVERED CARD STOCK FOR STABILITY.

WATERCOLOR LEMONS AND SILHOUETTE TO ENHANCE THE MESSAGE.

USE AN OPAQUE MARKING PEN TO ADD TRIOS OF DOTS FOR TEXTURE.

TYPE AND PRINT RECIPES FOR A CLEAN APPEARANCE.

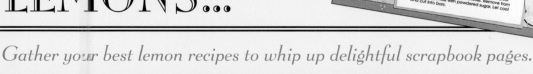

When Life Gives You Lemons... BAKE!

Grandma's Lemon Sponge
Cream 1 1 butter; 1 C sugar; grated rind of 1 lemon; 2 well-beaten egg yolks; 3 1 sifted flour; 1 C milk; juice of lemon. Beat egg whites and add to mixture.

Bake in pan of hot water in a 325 degree oven for 30–45 minutes.

Mom's Lemon Bisque
1 pkg. lemon jello
Juice and rind of 1 lemon
1 1/4 C hot water
1/2 C sugar

Cook and whip all ingredients. Whip 1 1/2 C cream; add to whipped jello mixture. Pour into pan lined with graham crackers. If desired, add pineapple and cherries. Put in refrigerator until ready to serve.

Gert's Lemon-Currant Bars
2 1 grated lemon rind
2 1/2 T lemon juice
1/3 C currants
1 1/2 C flour
1/2 t baking powder
1/2 C Crisco
1 C powdered sugar
1 large egg

Grease a 7×11-inch pan. Mix lemon rind, juice, and currants; let stand 15 minutes. Mix the remaining ingredients; add lemon mixture. Pour in greased pan and bake in a 350 degree oven for 25 minutes. Cook in pan on rack overnight.

Anndie's Lemon Bars
2 C plus 4 T flour
1 C butter
1/2 C powdered sugar
2 C granulated sugar
1 t baking powder
4 eggs, lightly beaten
4 T lemon juice
Grated rind of 1 lemon

Mix 2 cups flour, butter, and powdered sugar with pastry blender; pat in bottom of a 9×13-inch pan. Bake 20 minutes at 350 degrees. Combine sugar, 4 T flour and baking powder; add eggs. Blend in lemon juice and rind. Mix well and pour over hot crust. Bake for 25 minutes. Remove from oven and sprinkle with powdered sugar. Let cool and cut into bars.

WHEN LIFE GIVES YOU LEMONS...

Gather your best lemon recipes to whip up delightful scrapbook pages.

WHAT YOU NEED

Recipes; photos of cooks
8½×11-inch green check paper
8½×11-inch green print paper
Two 12-inch squares of turquoise card stock; white card stock
White paper; yellow paper
Watercolor paints in yellow and light orange; paintbrush
Letter stickers; scissors
Computer and printer
Opaque white pen
Adhesive

WHAT TO DO

1 Cut the green check and print papers in half to make 8½×5½-inch rectangles. Using the photos as guides, glue the check papers to the top of the turquoise papers and the print papers to the bottom.

2 Watercolor lemon shapes, using the pattern, *page 104,* as a guide for shape. Let dry. Cut out.

3 Use press-on lettering to write WHEN LIFE GIVES YOU LEMONS... BAKE! on the left-hand page.

4 Print lemon recipes on white paper. Trim each recipe and glue to yellow paper. Trim narrow yellow borders.

5 Crop circles from the photos. Glue recipes and photos on the pages.

6 Use a white pen to apply dots in groups of three to the turquoise paper.

COOKIE CUTTER, CIRCA 1950

MOTHER'S APPLE PIE

Vintage linens set the tone for these scrapbook pages devoted to the '50s.

WHAT YOU NEED

Recipes

Photo

Two 12-inch squares of red card stock

Card stock in blue, yellow, and black; white paper

Photocopied vintage tablecloth with figures

Paper cutter; scissors; ruler

Computer and printer

Adhesive

WHAT TO DO

1 Mount recipes on black card stock. Trim ⅛ inch beyond recipe cards.

2 Computer-generate a headline and journaling on white paper; crop. When producing journaling for old photos and recipes, such as these, include as much information and history as possible (read the journaling block, *below,* for ideas). Mount the journaling block to black card stock; trim, leaving ¼ inch at the top, ½ inch on each side, and 2 inches at the bottom. Mount the headline to 2½-inch-wide scallop-edge yellow card stock.

USE A HANDWRITTEN RECIPE FOR A PERSONAL TOUCH.

COMPUTER-GENERATE JOURNALING AND MOUNT ON BLACK.

PHOTOCOPY A VINTAGE TABLECLOTH TO REINFORCE A PERIOD OF TIME.

Mother's Apple Pie

Apple Pie
for a 2-crust 8-inch pie
6 cups sliced tart apples
1 t. lemon juice
¾C sugar
3 T flour
½ t. Cinnamon 1 T butter
dash salt
Mix all ingredients. Place in pie
shell - cover with top crust. Brush
with milk & sugar.
Bake 375° 25 mins
then 325° 25 mins

In 1955 Mother and Dad purchased one of the first home freezers in the area. This new purchase was the talk of the town. The local newspaper and TV station decided to make this event a story. The owner of the Hardware store, John Whyte, and Mother posed for this classic picture. Mother was noted for her delicious pies and now Dad could have them fresh from the freezer any time he wished. Mother proudly displays her famous Apple Pie.

FLOUR SIFTER, CIRCA 1950

From the photocopied tablecloth, cut a blue scalloped strip the width of the paper for the right-hand page.

3 Cut two large sections from the photocopy of a tablecloth, 6½×10 inches and 8×6 inches. Silhouette several small shapes from the tablecloth photocopy for embellishments.

4 Mount the photo on blue card stock; crop ⅛ inch beyond the edge of the photo.

5 Adhere the elements to the pages.

NEVERFAIL PIE CRUST

1 heaping c. lard   5 T. water
3 c. sifted flour   1 t. vinegar
1 egg beaten   1 t. salt

Cut lard into flour until it's in small
pieces. Add rest of ingredients to beaten
egg and mix into flour mixture. Makes two
2-crust pies. Dough will keep several days
if refrigerated.

USE AN ORIGINAL TYPED RECIPE FOR AUTHENTICITY.

SILHOUETTE PORTIONS OF PHOTOCOPIED TABLECLOTH.

MOUNT PHOTO TO CONTRAST FROM BACKGROUND.

FARM APPLE PIE

Papers in apple-fresh colors add to scrapbook pages devoted to a farm family favorite—apple pie.

WHAT YOU NEED

Recipes; photos

Two 12-inch squares of red card stock; card stock in red, green, and off-white speckle

Green vellum; tracing paper

Scrap metal, such as Once Upon A Scribble

Die cuts, farm and apple

Eyelets

Black alphabet stickers

Dimensional stickers, apple and kitchen themes

Vellum stickers, apple theme

Chalk in pink, green, and brown

Eyelet tool

Paper punch; scissors; pencil

Paper cutter; computer and printer; marking pens in black, brown, and red

Paper crimper, such as Fiskars

Adhesive foam mounts, such as Pop Dots; adhesive

WHAT TO DO

1 Crop photos and recipes as desired. Mount the photos, recipes, and farm die cut on green or red card stock. Double-mount, if desired, trimming just beyond the adjacent layer. Cut small green rectangles for sticker backgrounds.

MOUNT A DIE CUT TO CARD STOCK AND EMBELLISH WITH A DIMENSIONAL STICKER ON ONE OF THE LETTERS.

FRAME PHOTOS WITH NARROW BORDERS.

GROUP DIMENSIONAL STICKERS ON CARD STOCK RECTANGLES.

USE EYELETS TO ATTACH PIECES IN AN INTERESTING WAY.

3 Generations of pie making
Grandma Johnson
Mom & Jill
Oct. '02

HEADLINE IDEAS

1. *Grandma's Apple Pie*
2. *Pie from the Farm*
3. *Farm Girls Sure Do Bake!*
4. *Apple Pie to Die For!*
5. *Three Generations Make Pie*

2 Trace the pie pattern, *page 105.* Cut out the shapes. For the pie, use the pan pattern to cut a metal piece. Cut the pie crust from off-white speckle card stock. Randomly outline the crust edges, adding diagonal lines and inked areas to the crust. Crimp the crust edge piece.

Chalk a scrap of off-white paper. Tear four small shapes from inked paper to embellish the pie top. Adhere the pie to a background piece of card stock.

3 Place apple die cut on white card stock; trace shape. Print journaling in drawn shape; cut out. Use chalk to tint apple shape. Outline

with black marking pen. Define stem with brown.

4 Print a caption on green vellum. Tear the edges. Apply stickers to card stock pieces, around recipe, and on headline. Use marking pens to draw dashed lines around paper edges. Arrange torn vellum on a stickered paper, adhere with two eyelets. Mount to another piece of card stock.

5 Arrange pieces and adhere in place, using adhesive foam mounts where desired.

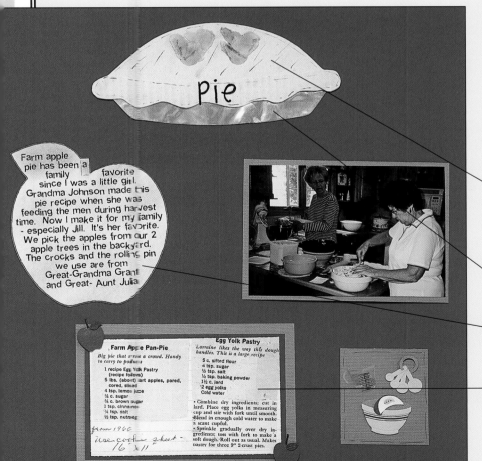

USE A PAPER CRIMPER TO ADD TEXTURE.

EASY-TO-CUT METAL ADDS A REALISTIC TOUCH.

USE CHALK TO ADD SUBTLE COLOR.

PHOTOCOPY RECIPES AND WRITTEN NOTES IN COLOR TO MAINTAIN PATINA.

ITTY-BITTY BOOKLET

For a small scrapbook, create mini pages that burst with composition and details. Choose the theme and let these grand ideas guide you in developing the pages.

WHAT YOU NEED FOR BOOKLET

Recipes; photos
5½×7¼-inch coordinating card
stock and print papers (or size
to fit sleeves in scrapbook)
Vellum; round brads
Round eyelets
Photo corners; paw stickers

Fiber; brown chalk
Computer and printer
Paper cutter; scissors; antique-edge
scissors; paper punch; eyelet tool
Adhesive foam mounts, such as
Pop Dots

Small leaf punch
Fine-line brown marking pen
Small cellophane bag
Adhesive

CHOOSE COLORS FROM BACKGROUND PAPER TO USE AS SOLID ACCENTS.

CUT MOUNTING PAPER WITH ANTIQUE-EDGE SCISSORS.

USE PHOTO CORNERS FOR A PROFESSIONAL FINISH.

THREAD FIBER THROUGH EYELETS AND TAGS TO CONNECT THEM.

HAND-CUT SHAPES FILL WHITE SPACE AND ADD INTEREST.

PRINT JOURNALING AND CUT A LARGE TAG; EMBELLISH WITH TORN PAPER AND EYELETS.

CUT AND PLACE PAPER SQUARES ON EACH PAGE CORNER TO ANCHOR PIECES.

Pumpkin Butter
Living History Farms

8 cups mashed pumpkin
6 - 8 cups sugar (to taste)
1 tablespoon cinnamon
1 teaspoon cloves
1 teaspoon ginger

Combine all ingredients. Simmer over low heat or in low oven until very thick. Process in jars or freeze.

A few years back, we went to a period dinner at the 1900 farm site of Living History Farms. I can still recall the warmth of the kitchen where dinner was served directly from the mammoth black stove. One of the wonderful new tastes we experienced was pumpkin butter served with fresh-baked rolls. The recipe was so good that we have made it for gifts. In this picture, Bailey helps a woman in the Tangen House with gingerbread cookies on one of our numerous visits to the farms.

Bailey, age 7, December, 2000

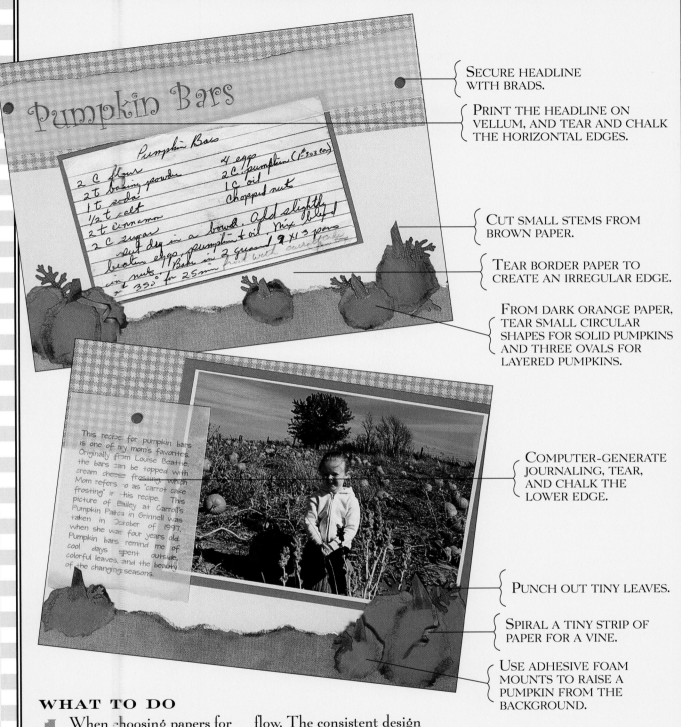

SECURE HEADLINE WITH BRADS.

PRINT THE HEADLINE ON VELLUM, AND TEAR AND CHALK THE HORIZONTAL EDGES.

CUT SMALL STEMS FROM BROWN PAPER.

TEAR BORDER PAPER TO CREATE AN IRREGULAR EDGE.

FROM DARK ORANGE PAPER, TEAR SMALL CIRCULAR SHAPES FOR SOLID PUMPKINS AND THREE OVALS FOR LAYERED PUMPKINS.

COMPUTER-GENERATE JOURNALING, TEAR, AND CHALK THE LOWER EDGE.

PUNCH OUT TINY LEAVES.

SPIRAL A TINY STRIP OF PAPER FOR A VINE.

USE ADHESIVE FOAM MOUNTS TO RAISE A PUMPKIN FROM THE BACKGROUND.

WHAT TO DO

1 When choosing papers for a mini scrapbook with pages that have continuity, purchase enough papers for the entire book. These page samples, *pages 24–29,* use papers that vary for each different entry; however, the prints and colors coordinate and make the pages flow. The consistent design element is the use of tan tones and horizontal stripes.

2 Crop the photos as desired. Single- or double-mount the photos on card stock.

3 To create the backgrounds, cut or tear papers and adhere in place using the photos for inspiration. Read the callouts by each page to note how to create each of the special effects.

continued on page 26

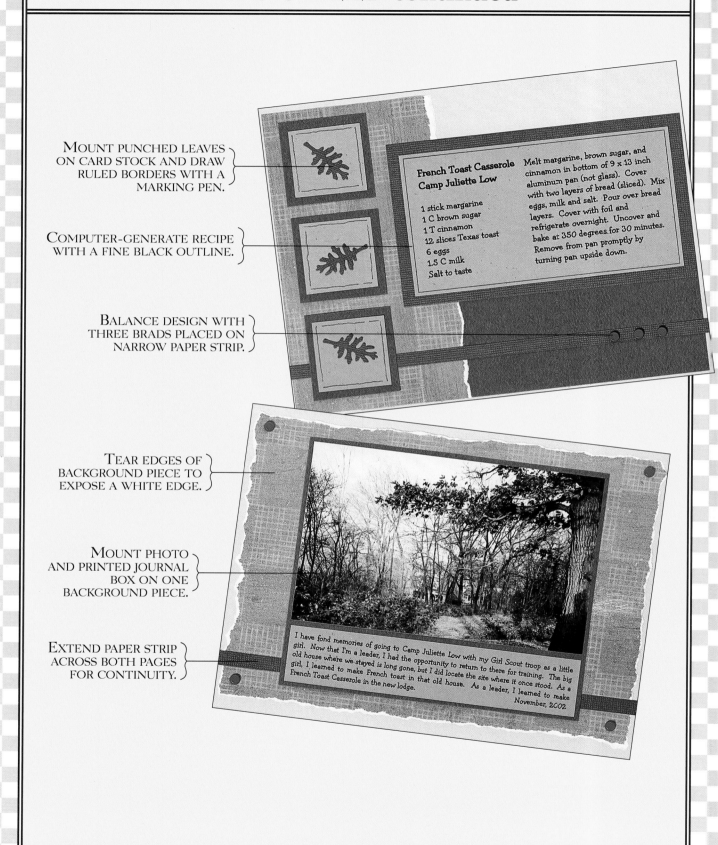

MOUNT PUNCHED LEAVES ON CARD STOCK AND DRAW RULED BORDERS WITH A MARKING PEN.

COMPUTER-GENERATE RECIPE WITH A FINE BLACK OUTLINE.

BALANCE DESIGN WITH THREE BRADS PLACED ON NARROW PAPER STRIP.

TEAR EDGES OF BACKGROUND PIECE TO EXPOSE A WHITE EDGE.

MOUNT PHOTO AND PRINTED JOURNAL BOX ON ONE BACKGROUND PIECE.

EXTEND PAPER STRIP ACROSS BOTH PAGES FOR CONTINUITY.

French Toast Casserole
Camp Juliette Low

1 stick margarine
1 C brown sugar
1 T cinnamon
12 slices Texas toast
6 eggs
1.5 C milk
Salt to taste

Melt margarine, brown sugar, and cinnamon in bottom of 9 x 13 inch aluminum pan (not glass). Cover with two layers of bread (sliced). Mix eggs, milk and salt. Pour over bread layers. Cover with foil and refrigerate overnight. Uncover and bake at 350 degrees for 30 minutes. Remove from pan promptly by turning pan upside down.

I have fond memories of going to Camp Juliette Low with my Girl Scout troop as a little girl. Now that I'm a leader, I had the opportunity to return to there for training. The big old house where we stayed is long gone, but I did locate the site where it once stood. As a girl, I learned to make French toast in that old house. As a leader, I learned to make French Toast Casserole in the new lodge.
November, 2002

HEADLINE IDEAS

1. *Grandma's Best Recipes*
2. *Times in the Kitchen are the BEST!*
3. *We Love to Bake*
4. *All Our Family's Favorites—Even the Dog's!*

CHILD'S PITCHER AND FORK, CIRCA 1910

Canine Crunchies

1 t instant beef bouillon
1/2 C hot water
3/4 C white flour
1.5 C wheat flour
1/2 C non-fat dry milk
1/3 C olive oil
3.25 ounces bacon flavored pieces
1 T packed brown sugar
1 egg

Combine bouillon and water and stir until dissolved. Stir in the remaining ingredients and mix well. Roll out dough to 1/2 inch thickness using a lightly floured rolling pin. Use cookie cutters to cut out dog biscuits and place on greased baking sheet. Bake at 300 degrees for 30-35 minutes or until firm. Cool on wire rack.

Leah & Bailey
December, 2002

EXTEND PAPER STRIP ACROSS BOTH PAGES FOR CONTINUITY.

MOUNT PAW STICKERS ON CARD STOCK AND DRAW RULED BORDERS WITH A MARKING PEN.

SILHOUETTE A PHOTO FOR ADDED IMPACT.

A few days before Christmas, Bailey and Leah Bowman baked and packaged dog biscuits and cat treats to give as gifts. Leah would like to sell packaged dog biscuits eventually, and Bailey had experience with creative packaging, so the two made a good team. The festive smell of beef bouillon wafted through the kitchen as the girls baked huge batches. Feedback from gift recipients was positive, except for one minor incident where a neighborhood cat almost choked on one of the treats. (Next time, the treats will be cut much into much smaller bites!)

PLACE TORN PAPER IN A SMALL CELLOPHANE BAG AND ADD A PAPER TOPPER COMPLETE WITH A PRINTED LABEL.

TACK VELLUM JOURNAL BOX IN PLACE WITH COORDINATING EYELETS.

ANGLE VELLUM FOR INTEREST.

continued on page 28

PAPER ATTACHED
WITH BRADS ADDS
AN ARTSY TOUCH.

PHOTOCOPY BOTH SIDES
OF ORIGINAL RECIPE, TRIM,
MOUNT, AND PLACE
OVERLAPPED ON PAGE.

PRINT HEADLINE ON VELLUM
AND CHALK THE EDGES.

CARRY THE STRIPE
PAPER TO THE SECOND
PAGE BY PLACING A
STRIP AT THE TOP.

MOUNT DARK PHOTOS
ON LIGHT COLORS TO
MAKE THEM POP.

MAINTAIN THE DATE
ON PHOTOS FOR
FUTURE REFERENCE.

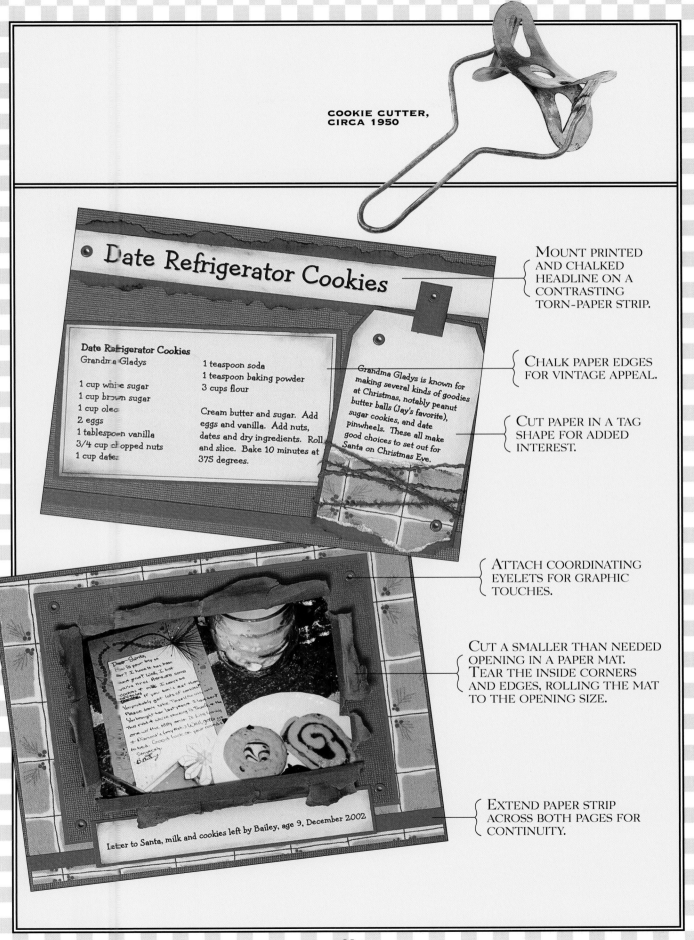

COOKIE CUTTER,
CIRCA 1950

Date Refrigerator Cookies

Date Refrigerator Cookies
Grandma Gladys

1 cup white sugar
1 cup brown sugar
1 cup oleo
2 eggs
1 tablespoon vanilla
3/4 cup chopped nuts
1 cup dates

1 teaspoon soda
1 teaspoon baking powder
3 cups flour

Cream butter and sugar. Add eggs and vanilla. Add nuts, dates and dry ingredients. Roll and slice. Bake 10 minutes at 375 degrees.

Grandma Gladys is known for making several kinds of goodies at Christmas, notably peanut butter balls (Jay's favorite), sugar cookies, and date pinwheels. These all make good choices to set out for Santa on Christmas Eve.

MOUNT PRINTED AND CHALKED HEADLINE ON A CONTRASTING TORN-PAPER STRIP.

CHALK PAPER EDGES FOR VINTAGE APPEAL.

CUT PAPER IN A TAG SHAPE FOR ADDED INTEREST.

ATTACH COORDINATING EYELETS FOR GRAPHIC TOUCHES.

CUT A SMALLER THAN NEEDED OPENING IN A PAPER MAT. TEAR THE INSIDE CORNERS AND EDGES, ROLLING THE MAT TO THE OPENING SIZE.

EXTEND PAPER STRIP ACROSS BOTH PAGES FOR CONTINUITY.

Letter to Santa, milk and cookies left by Bailey, age 9, December 2002

GRANDMA'S COOKIES

Celebrate the cook in your family and favorite recipes with a clever page filled with motifs from a vintage towel.

WHAT YOU NEED

Recipes on cards; photo
12-inch squares of white
  background paper
Vintage kitchen towel
5 print background papers to
  coordinate with towel
8½×11-inch white paper
8½×11-inch parchment paper
Wooden fork and spoon
  (toy- or full-size)
White crafting foam
Silver alphabet stickers
Scissors; decorative-edge scissors
Paper cutter; ruler
Adhesive

WHAT TO DO

1 To make the background that ties the pages together, choose three coordinating print papers. Cut the top and bottom strips for each page 11×4½ inches and the center strip 11×2 inches. Adhere the strips across the spread, centering the papers to allow the white background to frame the pages.

2 The paper with the marching characters is a vintage kitchen towel color photocopied. If you need to reverse the direction of the

CROP PHOTO IN AN OVAL AND MOUNT TO A CHECK BACKGROUND WITH DECORATIVE BORDER.

PHOTOCOPY KITCHEN UTENSILS, SILHOUETTE, AND MOUNT ON FOAM PIECES.

PHOTOCOPY A VINTAGE TOWEL OR TABLECLOTH TO CREATE INTERESTING BACKGROUNDS.

COOKIE CUTTER, CIRCA 1940

images, as on the right-hand page, photocopy using a mirror image setting. Silhouette some of the characters to accent them. If you don't have a vintage towel, check antiques stores and flea markets for a towel or piece of vintage fabric.

Reproductions also are available at discount and fabric stores.

3 To maintain the worn look on the recipe cards, photocopy them in color and trim them to resemble the worn corners.

4 To create headlines, adhere silver alphabet stickers on white paper rectangles. Mount the white rectangles to print paper and trim ⅛-inch borders. Mount the headline to parchment paper and trim it with decorative-edge scissors.

5 Crop the portrait in an oval and double-mat it. Photocopy a wooden spoon and fork. If using full-size utensils, reduce the size to fit the page. Silhouette the pieces and mount them to strips of foam.

6 Adhere the elements in place.

REVERSE IMAGES WHEN NECESSARY TO MAKE A PLEASING LAYOUT.

CUT PRINT PAPERS TO FORM CONTINUOUS HORIZONTAL BANDS.

HIS & HERS

Everyone has a favorite meal. Here's an ingenious way to remember a husband's and wife's most loved—1970s style!

WHAT YOU NEED

Recipes; 2 wallet-size photos

Two 12-inch squares of white card stock

12×18-inch black and metallic gold stripe paper

12×18-inch cream and metallic gold stripe paper

8-inch square of white paper

Cream-color lace stickers

Decorative pink paper borders

Dimensional floral sticker, such as Jolee's

Metallic gold alphabet stickers

Press-on gems, pearls, and metallic gold dots

2 black buttons

Ornate gold and pink button

Ruler; scissors

Paper cutter; pencil

Thick white crafts glue

Black fine-line marking pen

Adhesive

WHAT TO DO

1 To make a jacket or dress top, cut a 12-inch square from stripe paper. With stripes running vertically, make a pencil mark 2 inches from the top and 4 inches from side edge. If making both the HIS and HERS pages, make the marks on opposite sides of the papers. Use a ruler

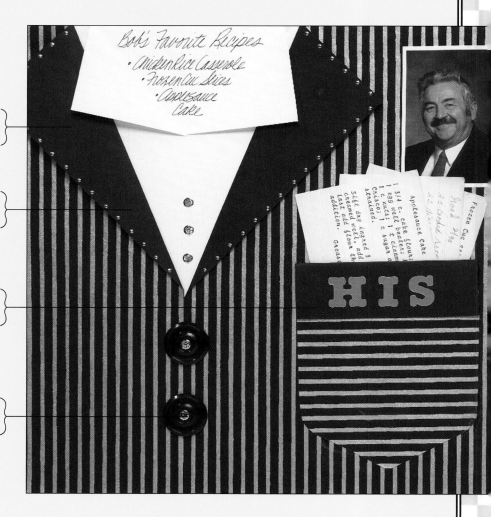

CREATE MIRROR IMAGES FOR A BALANCED SPREAD.

A SINGLE VERTICAL CUT ENABLES THE PAPER TO BE FOLDED BACK FOR LAPELS.

A POCKET EASILY HOLDS UP TO TEN RECIPE CARDS.

USE CRAFTS GLUE TO HOLD BUTTONS FIRMLY IN PLACE.

MUSTARD
JAR,
CIRCA
1920

to draw 7 inches down from the mark. Cut along line with scissors. Fold back the paper edges to make lapels. Trim lapels that extend beyond the edge.

2 For the shirt collar under the black stripe jacket, use an 8-inch square of white paper. Mark and cut 3 inches down the center of one side.

Glue under jacket; fold back collar points.

3 Glue both striped pieces to a 12-inch square of white card stock. Trace the pocket pattern, *page 106;* cut out. Cut a pocket from each remaining stripe paper. Fold cuff; glue.

4 Adhere only the side and bottom edges of the pocket to background.

5 For the dress, glue the pink borders at the neck edge and on the pocket. Press on lace, gems, pearls, and dot accents as shown. Adhere the floral sticker to the HERS lapel. Glue the buttons in place using crafts glue.

6 Write journaling on white background paper to show at the top of each page. Place recipe cards in the pockets.

PRESS-ON GEMS MAKE
INTERESTING DETAILS.

LACE STICKERS ADD
A FEMININE TOUCH.

SHARON TURNS THREE

In honor of a birthday past, recycle greeting cards that coordinate with photos to make pretty mats. Dainty print papers continue the pastel theme of these pages.

WHAT YOU NEED

Recipe
Photos
Two 12-inch squares of
  print paper
Greeting cards
Coordinating paper for headline
  and journaling
Paper with 12-inch-long pattern
  to trim the pages and cake photo
Solid coordinating paper

Small metal frame
¼-inch-wide sheer ribbon
Alphabet stickers
Paper cutter
Computer and printer
Adhesive

WHAT TO DO

1 Crop the photos as desired. To make photo mats or mounting papers, choose print greeting cards in colors that coordinate with the photos. Photocopy the cards, adjusting the sizes as needed. To make a mat, either cut an opening in the photocopy or

TIE NARROW SHEER RIBBON
BOWS FOR A DAINTY TOUCH.

MAKE AN ENLARGED
PHOTOCOPY OF THE
CARD IF DESIRED.

FRAME A CAKE PHOTO
WITH A DECORATIVE BORDER
AND PAPER CANDLES.

A SMALL METAL FRAME ADDS
DIMENSION AND INTEREST.

HEADLINE IDEAS

1. *Happy Birthday Memories*
2. *My Favorite Cake When I Was 3*
3. *My Ballerina Cake*
4. *Happy Birthday to Me!*
5. *I'm a Ballerina, and My Cake Is Too*

adhere the photo on the mat. Silhouette small details from cards to embellish the pages.

2 Computer-generate journaling and a recipe, printing them in a color to coordinate with the photos and papers. Crop them irregularly and mount to coordinating

paper or card photocopies. Trim as desired.

3 Silhouette a 12-inch design to border the top of the pages, such as the diamond shapes, *below*.

4 Mount a photo of the cake on solid paper. Trim a ¼-inch border. Round the top corners. Cut and adhere paper

details and candles.

5 Crop a photo to fit the small metal frame. Adhere in place.

6 For the headline, cut ¾-inch squares from coordinating print paper, enough to back each letter. Press alphabet stickers on squares and adhere them to the page on point. Adhere the remaining elements in place.

7 Tie two generous bows from ribbon and adhere to photos.

RECYCLE GREETING CARDS TO MAKE PRETTY PHOTO MATS AND MOUNTING PAPERS.

PRINT JOURNALING IN A COORDINATING COLOR AND CROP IRREGULARLY.

CELEBRATING WITH RECIPES

When people gather—for holidays, parties, or any celebration—capture the events on film. Combine the photos with recipes of the food served and you'll always remember the special get-togethers. This chapter has creative ideas for an array of celebrations—from out-of-the-country vacations to birthday parties and the Fourth of July!

DINNER FOR TWELVE

Whether cooking for 2 or 12, preparing for a dinner party makes a great memory to record in a scrapbook.

WHAT YOU NEED

Recipes

Photos

Two 12-inch squares of royal blue card stock

Two 12-inch squares of Asian-inspired print papers

8½×11-inch papers in metallic gold and red

Three 3-inch-long off-white satin tassels; cording to match

Metallic gold calligraphy marking pen

Pencil; tape

Paper cutter

Scissors

Thick white crafts glue

Adhesive

WHAT TO DO

1 Crop the photos as desired. Mount the photos and recipe cards on metallic gold paper and trim narrow borders on each. Double-mount the recipe cards on metallic red, if desired, and trim a narrow border.

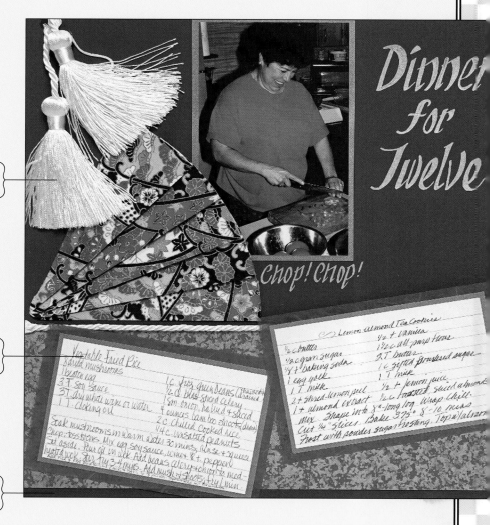

USE CORDED TASSELS TO ADD DIMENSION.

PHOTOCOPY ORIGINAL RECIPES, INCLUDING THE BACK SIDES IF NECESSARY.

LEAVE A STRIP OF BACKGROUND PAPER SHOWING AT THE BOTTOM EDGES.

HEADLINE IDEAS

1. *Dinner with a Flair of the Orient*
2. *Getting Ready for the Party*
3. *A Dozen for Dinner*
4. *Chop! Chop!*
5. *The Guests Are on Their Way*

CONTEMPORARY RICE BOWL

2 Cut two 4-inch-wide strips from Asian-inspired print paper for bottom of pages. Adhere to blue card stock.

3 For a pair of fans, draw an 11-inch-diameter circle on the back of a paper. Cut out the circle. Cut the circle in half. Fold each paper back and forth to make five pleats that extend from the center point. Tape the pleats in place on the back.

4 Arrange the photos, recipes, and fans on the background paper. Adhere the pieces in place. Use crafts glue to adhere cording along the upper edge of the wide bottom border, skipping over photos and recipes. Glue tassels in place. Let the glue dry.

5 Write a headline and journaling using a gold calligraphy pen.

PLEAT A HALF-CIRCLE TO MAKE A FAN.

USE METALLIC GOLD JOURNALING FOR AN ELEGANT TOUCH.

FAMILY REUNION

When this family gathers around a campfire, there's certain to be good conversation, lots of "remember when" laughs, and awesome home cookin'.

WHAT YOU NEED

Recipe; photos

Two 12-inch natural-tone background papers with borders

Outdoor-theme paper in dark green and tan

Card stock in tan, dark green, and off-white

Camping-theme stickers

Stick-style alphabet stickers

White crafting foam

Small sticks

Colored pencils in brown and black

Pen with disappearing ink

Computer and printer

Scissors; ruler

Oval cutter; paper cutter

Foam tape

Adhesive

WHAT TO DO

1 Crop the photos as desired. Mount the photos on paper or cut an oval mat from one of the solid papers, leaving from 1/16 to 1/2 inch of mats showing. For interest, cut a couple of mats in half

CENTER A STICKER IN THE HEADLINE COPY.

USE A PEN WITH DISAPPEARING INK TO DRAW A CIRCULAR GUIDE FOR HEADLINE.

CUT PAPERS IN HALF HORIZONTALLY FOR A TWIST ON MOUNTING.

ADD A STICKER BORDER THAT RELATES TO THE THEME OF THE PAGE.

HEADLINE IDEAS

1. *Grilled Tomatoes*
2. *Camping Out with Family*
3. *Our Favorite Reunion Recipe*
4. *Tomatoes...Grill-Style*
5. *Together at the Lake*

HOT DOG SKEWERS, CIRCA 1960

horizontally and glue to the lower half of the photo.

2 Print recipe on off-white paper. Trim, leaving approximately 1 inch around each edge. For character, carefully burn the edges of the paper.

3 To make the marshmallows, cut two wavy-edge rectangles from white crafting foam to measure $1\frac{1}{2} \times 1\frac{3}{4}$ inches. Use foam tape to adhere marshmallows to sticks.

4 Use a pen with disappearing ink to draw

a circular guide for headline stickers. Adhere the recipe, photos, marshmallows, and stickers in place.

GRILLED TOMATOES

CUT TOMATOES IN HALF. BRUSH CUT SURFACES WITH BOTTLED ITALIAN SALAD DRESSING; SPRINKLE WITH SALT, PEPPER, AND DRIED BASIL, CRUSHED. HEAT, CUT SIDE UP, ON ALUMINUM FOIL OR GREASED GRILL OVER HOT COALS ABOUT 10 MINUTES OR TILL HOT THROUGH (DON'T TURN).

CAREFULLY BURN THE EDGES OF THE RECIPE.

SMUDGE CRAFTING FOAM SHAPES WITH BLACK AND BROWN FOR A REALISTIC LOOK.

LOBSTER LUNCH IN MEXICO

When you discover new destinations and their cuisines, check your souvenir bag for motifs to reproduce as scrapbook trims.

WHAT YOU NEED

Recipe
Photos
Two 12-inch squares of stripe scrapbook paper
Card stock in colors to coordinate with stripe paper
Tracing paper
Woven place mat for hat
Alphabet stickers
Tape; paper cutter; scissors
Marking pens; pencil
Computer and printer
Thick white crafts glue
Adhesive

WHAT TO DO

1 To create quadrants from striped paper, cut each sheet in four equal squares. Rotate two opposite corner squares. Tape the papers together on the back side.

CUT A HAT SHAPE FROM A WOVEN PLACE MAT FOR TEXTURE.

CHOOSE A STICKER ALPHABET THAT CARRIES OUT THE THEME.

SILHOUETTE ONE OR TWO PHOTOS FOR INTEREST.

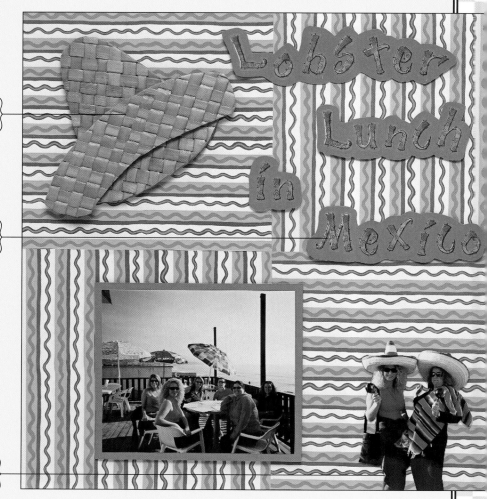

SOMBRERO PARTY FAVOR

2 Computer-generate and print a recipe on white paper. Crop the photos as desired, silhouetting some. Mount all but the silhouetted photos to card stock. Trim ⅛-inch narrow borders.

3 Use stickers to spell LOBSTER LUNCH IN MEXICO, or other headline, on card stock. Use scissors to trim around words.

4 To make a hat, trace the pattern, *page 107,* and cut out. Use the pattern to cut shapes from a place mat. Adhere the pieces together with crafts glue.

5 For maracas, trace the pattern, *page 105,* and cut out. Use the pattern to cut maracas from card stock. Use marking pens to draw stripes on the shaker section and to color in the handles.

6 Adhere all the elements in place.

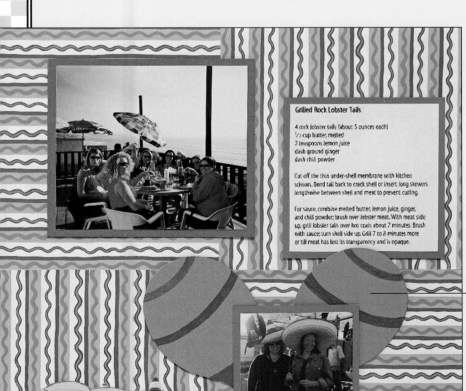

Grilled Rock Lobster Tails

4 rock lobster tails (about 5 ounces each)
½ cup butter, melted
2 teaspoons lemon juice
dash ground ginger
dash chili powder

Cut off the thin under-shell membrane with kitchen scissors. Bend tail back to crack shell or insert long skewers lengthwise between shell and meat to prevent curling.

For sauce, combine melted butter, lemon juice, ginger, and chili powder; brush over lobster meat. With meat side up, grill lobster tails over hot coals about 7 minutes. Brush with sauce; turn shell side up. Grill 7 to 8 minutes more or till meat has lost its transparency and is opaque.

USE MARKING PENS TO DETAIL PAPER MARACAS.

CUT STRIPED PAPER IN FOUR SQUARES AND REASSEMBLE FOR A BACKGROUND WITH MOVEMENT.

HAPPY NEW YEAR

No matter what you're celebrating, get your clues for creative pages from this whimsical arrangement.

WHAT YOU NEED

Recipe; photos

Two 12-inch squares of lavender and aqua swirls and stars scrapbook paper

Coordinating paper in rose

Card stock in black, silver, white, and glittery silver

Stickers with a New Year's theme

Curling ribbon in gold, pink, and purple

Silver alphabet stickers

Confetti and streamer stickers in silver and gold

Corner edger; paper cutter

Scissors; circle cutter; ruler

Hole punches in a variety of sizes

Black fine-line marking pen

Adhesive

WHAT TO DO

1 Crop photos as desired. Use a circle cutter to cut several circular crops. Use a corner edger to make ornate corner cuts. For the photos on the stemmed glasses, make a paper pattern, following the shape of the party glasses. Cut

USE HOLE PUNCHES TO MAKE BUBBLES.

USE A CIRCLE CUTTER FOR PRECISION CIRCLES.

TRIM PHOTOS TO NEST INSIDE PAPER SHAPES.

MAT PIECES IN THE COORDINATING PAPER, EDGING THE CORNERS.

REINFORCE THE THEME USING STICKERS.

PUNCH BOWL LADLE, CIRCA 1970

out the pattern. Trace around the bowl of the glass pattern on two photos. Cut out slightly smaller than traced lines. Use the pattern to cut stems from black and the bowl portion from glittery silver paper.

2 Cut black and silver bubbles using hole punches.

3 To make the horn, cut a long narrow triangle. Cut off the tip. For the opening at the wide end, cut a white paper oval to fit; glue it in place. Curl a few short pieces of curling ribbon. Glue to end of horn.

4 To make the scroll for the recipe, cut a 5½-inch

square from coordinating paper. Use a marking pen to write the recipe on the paper. Curl under the top and bottom of the paper using a pencil. Cut two 6½-inch-long strips from black. Curl under the top and bottom of the scroll. Thread a black strip through each curled end. Glue a punched hole on each end of the black paper strips.

5 Starting with the black triangles, adhere all pieces in place. Add stickers where desired.

Champagne Punch

Combine two 12 oz. cans of pineapple juice; 1 - 6 oz. can orange juice; one 6 oz. can lemonade; and 4 c. water. Chill thoroughly. Just before serving, transfer to punch bowl. Pour 4/5 qt. bottles champagne gently in bo

ROLL UNDER PAPER ENDS TO MAKE A SCROLL.

BOLD TRIANGLES ANCHOR DESIGN ELEMENTS.

CUT SILHOUETTES FROM PHOTOS FOR IMPACT.

OSCAR NIGHT

While this award-winning page has an Oscar night theme, you could easily adapt it to any festive gathering.

WHAT YOU NEED

Recipe

Photos

12-inch square and scraps of black card stock

Two 8½×11-inch sheets of white card stock

Papers in metallic red and gold

2½-inch-wide red satin ribbon

Photocopy of Oscar statue, approximately 7 inches high

Metallic gold star and alphabet stickers

Computer and printer

Paper cutter

Scissors; ruler

Circle cutter

Adhesive

WHAT TO DO

1 Silhouette people photos and crop food shots as desired. Mount food shots on gold paper and trim just beyond photo.

INCLUDE STAR STICKERS TO ADD MOVEMENT TO THE PAGE.

SILHOUETTE PHOTOS OF PEOPLE TO RESEMBLE ACTRESSES WALKING ON A RUNWAY.

PAPER CIRCLES WITH RIBBON TAILS MAKE EASY NOMINATION ENVELOPE SEALS.

USE SATIN RIBBON FOR THE RUNWAY.

MAKE TRI-FOLD ENVELOPES WITH PAPER SEALS FOR CONFIDENTIALITY.

2 Glue a ribbon diagonally across the background paper. Trim the ribbon ends even with the paper.

3 For the BEST OSCAR PARTY DISH card, print a recipe in a 2×3-inch rectangle, adding decorative graphics if desired. Center and print the recipe on white card stock. Trim card stock to measure 9¼×4½, centering the recipe. Make a mark 3 inches from the bottom. Make a second mark 3¾ inches from the first mark. Trim the paper 1½ inches beyond the last mark. Fold toward center at marked areas.

4 For the BEST DRESSED PARTYGOER card, print the winner's name in the center of a sheet of white card stock. Trim the paper to 2×3½ inches with the winner's name 1¾ inches from the top. Make a mark 1¼ inches from the bottom. Make a second mark 1¼ inches from the first mark. Fold at marked lines.

5 Computer-generate the banner along with ...AND THE WINNER IS... copy. Mount and frame the shape. Print the envelope captions, mount on black, and trim narrow borders.

6 To make the seals, cut circles from metallic red paper. Add two ribbon tails to each paper seal.

7 Using the photo as a guide, adhere elements in place. Press on the sticker headline and stars.

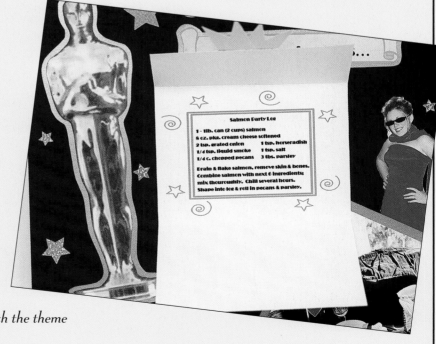

Print the recipe on the inside of the folded card to blend with the theme of the page.

PRETZEL PARTY

Assembled using Christmas colors, this family tradition of dipping pretzels is captured in a graphic composition.

WHAT YOU NEED

Recipe
Photos
Two 12-inch squares of green
  card stock
12-inch square of white card stock
12-inch square of red card stock
2-inch-high alphabet punch
8 red square brads
Paper cutter
Computer and printer
Adhesive

WHAT TO DO

1 Crop the photos as desired and mount on white card stock. Trim narrow borders.

2 Using small lettering, computer-generate the journaling and recipes. Print copy on white and trim to size.

Mount on red card stock and trim narrow borders.

3 Photocopy a photo of the pretzels, enlarging and copying it several times for adequate space to punch the headline and to trim the lower edges of the pages. Punch the letters and cut strips from the

BOLD LETTERING MAKES
A HEADLINE WITH IMPACT.

INCLUDE SOME CLOSE-UP
SHOTS TO SHOW DETAIL.

CUT AN ENLARGED
PHOTO INTO STRIPS FOR
A GRAPHIC LOOK.

What a blast we had when Mom came out to spend the day with us cooking up special treats. A favorite of everyone's is the almond bark coated pretzels. We all got a big laugh when Diane drug out her eyebrow tweezers to dip the pretzels in the almond bark. She assured us it was sterilized!
November 2002

HEADLINE IDEAS
....

1. *Making Pretzels for Christmas*
2. *Candy-Coating Pretzels*
3. *Having a Merry Ol' Time*
4. *Merrymaking in the Kitchen*
5. *Christmas Pretzel Party*

SLOTTED SPOON, CIRCA 1920

copies. Mount the letters on red card stock, trim narrow borders. Cut two 12×3½-inch strips from red card stock. Cut six 12×1-inch strips from photo enlargement. Glue three photo strips to each red card stock strip, leaving approximately ⅛ inch between strips.

4 Cut two 12×3-inch strips from white card stock for the headline. Adhere all pieces in place.

5 Place a square brad in each corner of the headline background.

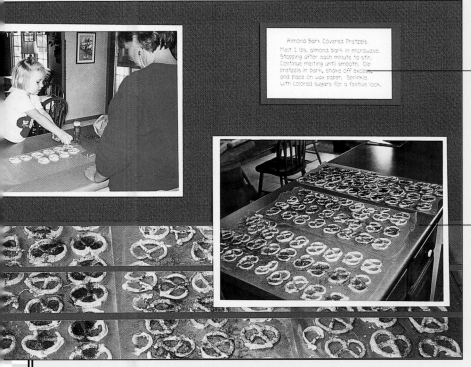

Almond Bark Covered Pretzels

Melt 2 lbs. almond bark in microwave, stopping after each minute to stir. Continue melting until smooth. Dip pretzels in bark, shake off excess, and place on wax paper. Sprinkle with colored sugars for a festive look.

USE BRADS TO ADD DIMENSION AND INTEREST.

COMPUTER-GENERATE JOURNALING AND RECIPE FOR A NEAT APPEARANCE.

INCLUDE PHOTOS OF THE FINISHED PROJECT TO HELP RECALL THE MEMORY.

FOURTH OF JULY

Almost as exciting as fireworks, this scrapbook design sparkles with pride for the red, white, and blue.

WHAT YOU NEED

Recipe
Photos
Two 12-inch squares of white with metallic blue stars and confetti scrapbook paper
12×4-inch piece of red card stock
Card stock in metallic red, metallic blue, and silver glitter
Small fabric flag on pole
Red, white, and blue star garland decoration
Small plastic flag
Fireworks stickers
Star template
Black alphabet stickers
Paper cutter
Decorative-edge scissors
Corner rounder
Oval cutter
Computer and printer
Adhesive

WHAT TO DO

1 Crop photos using a corner rounder and an oval cutter.

2 Mount each photo on metallic blue or red paper and trim narrow borders.

3 Print a recipe from a computer, adding a flag

A SMALL FABRIC FLAG ADDS DIMENSION.

USE AN OVAL CUTTER TO CROP PHOTOS AND MOUNTING PAPER.

USE ALPHABET STICKERS TO LABEL THE PAGE QUICKLY.

A SOLID-COLOR STRIP ACCENTS THE BUSY BACKGROUND.

HEADLINE IDEAS
....

1. *Independence Day Fun*
2. *Fun on the Fourth*
3. *My Pick of the Picnic*
4. *Favorite Fourth of July Recipe*
5. *Getting Together on the Fourth*

**CHILD'S
PICNIC
BASKET,
CIRCA 1930**

background if desired. Crop recipe and mount on metallic paper.

4 Cut a 1½-inch-wide wavy strip from red card stock using decorative-edge scissors for the vertical border on the left-hand page. Use the star template to make various sizes of stars. Layer two large stars to anchor each page. Cut a long, narrow triangle from metallic blue paper.

5 Using the photo as a guide, adhere the red strip, photos, recipe, and blue triangle in place. Adhere a large layered star at the bottom of the triangle, leaving the top edge open. Place ends of garland decoration and plastic flag between the star and triangle. Glue in place.

6 Glue the stars and the flag in place. Adhere 4TH OF JULY on three red stars. Press fireworks stickers on the red paper border strip.

SEPARATE TRIMS FROM THE BACKGROUND WITH A LARGE PAPER TRIANGLE.

COMPUTER-GENERATE A RECIPE, ADDING FLAG GRAPHICS TO THE BACKGROUND.

USE A TEMPLATE TO CUT OUT PERFECT STARS.

BLUE CHEESE BURGERS

2 lbs. ground beef
1/3 c. chopped onion
1/2 c. crumbled blue cheese
2 tsp. salt
1 tbsp. Worcestershire sauce

Combine all ingredients. Shape mixture into 10 round patties. Grill 5 - 6 minutes; turn and grill additional 5 minutes.

FROM THIS MOMENT ON

A wedding day is full of wonderful memories, including the delicious cake that is shared.

WHAT YOU NEED

Recipe; photos

Two 12-inch squares of dark red card stock

12-inch square of coordinating floral card stock

Cream card stock

8½×11-inch piece of coordinating print scrapbook paper

Scrap of musical note paper

Invitation

1 yard of 1½-inch-wide floral ribbon

Computer-generated recipe printed with heart border

Die cuts of small hearts and a large wine bottle

Small dimensional wine bottles, glasses, grapes, satin ribbon bows with roses, and wedding rings

Paper cutter

Decorative-edge scissors

Corner rounder; scissors

Oval cutter

Computer and printer

Adhesive

WHAT TO DO

1 Crop photos using a corner rounder and an oval cutter. Use scissors to cut silhouettes. Cut an oval in the print paper for a mat. Use the cutout to mount a silhouette. Cut small fan shapes from print paper scraps for page corners.

PRECUT SHAPES ADD A LOVELY LACY TOUCH.

USE AN OVAL CUTTER TO CREATE MATS.

EMBELLISHMENTS CARRY OUT THE THEME AND ADD DIMENSION.

CAKE
DECORATOR,
CIRCA 1960

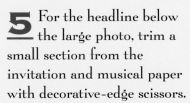

HEADLINE IDEAS

1. *Our Wedding ...Our Cake*
2. *Have Your Cake and Eat It Too*
3. *Wedding Day Memories*
4. *The Day That Took the Cake*
5. *Unforgettable*

2 Mount the desired photos and trim the borders evenly.

3 To add a ribbon border, such as the large floral-print border around the photo on the left-hand page, cut the ribbon into four pieces, 2½ inches longer than the mat

sides, top, and bottom measurements. Notch the ribbon ends. Overlap ribbon ends to make a frame; glue in place behind large matted photo.

4 Print recipe on cream card stock, adding a heart border. Mount on dark red card stock; trim a narrow border.

5 For the headline below the large photo, trim a small section from the invitation and musical paper with decorative-edge scissors.

6 Adhere the die cuts, photos, and remaining embellishments in place.

CUT SILHOUETTES TO ADD INTEREST.

COMPUTER-GENERATE A RECIPE FOR A PROFESSIONAL LOOK.

BY THE SEA

Sanded, torn, and crumpled, this interesting mix of papers makes a beautifully textured background for a favorite by-the-sea salad recipe.

Affix the recipe under the paper flap.

WHAT YOU NEED

Recipe; photo
12-inch square of card stock
12-inch square of metallic blue paper
Papers in gold metallic and shades of blue
Sandpaper
24-gauge white crafting wire
Photo of flag; starfish die cuts
Small shells; foam tape
Paper cutter; scissors; ruler
Permanent blue marking pen
Thick white crafts glue
Tape; adhesive

WHAT TO DO

1 Cut the metallic blue paper to 8×12 inches. Crumple and smooth out. Adhere to the card stock for sky.

2 Tear pieces of blue paper for waves. Adhere below crumpled-paper sky. Tear gold paper for sand; adhere below waves. Tear two additional pieces of gold to make a flap to cover recipe area along lower right-hand corner. Tape edge of flap to the back of card stock.

3 For sand castle, cut a 5½-inch square, a triangle, and six ½×1-inch pieces from sandpaper. Tear several small irregular pieces. Assemble and adhere the sand castle to background. Adhere photo in place. Use foam tape to add torn pieces at the bottom.

4 Cut a flag from a photo. Glue flag, paper starfish, and shells in place.

5 Shape pieces of wire to read BY THE SEA. Use crafts glue to adhere to sky area.

6 Write or adhere the recipe under the flap.

Cut a flag from a photo for the crowning touch.

Crumple metallic paper for a textured sky.

Cut and tear sandpaper to make a sand castle.

Tear paper to expose edges for waves and sand.

Hide recipe under a torn-paper flap.

Combine paper die cuts with real shells for added detail.

Use foam tape to raise desired areas.

HAPPY BIRTHDAY

Bright colors and a geometric design are delightful for a birthday celebration.

USE A STENCIL TO CUT BALLOON SHAPES.

PHOTOCOPY FABRICS FOR A COLORFUL BACKGROUND.

USE EMBROIDERY FLOSS FOR BALLOON STRINGS.

CUT TWO 6-INCH SQUARES FROM EACH PRINT AND PLACE IN OPPOSITE CORNERS.

TRIM BORDERS WITH DECORATIVE-EDGE SCISSORS.

WHAT YOU NEED

Recipe
Photos
2 coordinating bright fabrics
4 solid coordinating colors of card
  stock
Balloon stencil
Embroidery floss
Alphabet stickers
Pencil
Paper cutter
Scissors
Decorative-edge scissors
Ruler
Computer and printer
Tape
Adhesive

WHAT TO DO

1 Crop photos as desired. Mount photos on solid card stock. Trim ¼ inch beyond photo edges using decorative-edge scissors.

2 Photocopy both fabrics. Cut two 6-inch squares from each print. Arrange the prints in opposite corners and tape together on the back.

3 Computer-generate a recipe to fit a 2×3-inch rectangle. Crop recipe, cutting the sides using decorative-edge scissors. Mount on contrasting

solid card stock; trim, rounding the corners.

4 Use the stencil to cut three balloon shapes. Arrange balloons and tape together on the back. Tape a length of embroidery floss to the bottom of each balloon. Use alphabet stickers for headline.

5 Adhere pieces in place, tucking the ends of the embroidery floss under the recipe block.

HOUSEWARMING FIESTA

With homemade guacamole dip the hit of this gathering, these pages come alive with Mexicana.

WHAT YOU NEED

Recipe; photos
12-inch squares of yellow
  print paper
Papers in orange, turquoise,
  green, yellow, purple, and red
Tracing paper
Primary-color fibers
1/4-inch-wide orange ribbon
Stickers, decorative-edge, guitar,
  and alphabet
Decorative-edge scissors; scissors
Paper cutter; pencil
Adhesive

WHAT TO DO

1 Crop the photos as desired and mount on turquoise paper rectangles or triangles. If desired, trim the top edge with decorative-edge scissors.

2 Cut two blanket shapes from orange paper. From remaining bright papers, cut and glue shapes on the blankets. Cut 1-inch-long pieces of fiber. Glue the fibers on the back of each narrow end of the blankets.

3 For the sombrero, trace the pattern on *page 107;*

USE FIBER STRANDS TO ADD COLORFUL DRAPES TO THE TOP OF EACH PAGE.

CUT A VARIETY OF SHAPES TO EMBELLISH A PAPER BLANKET.

MOUNT PHOTOS TO SOLID TRIANGLES FOR AN INTERESTING EFFECT.

HEADLINE IDEAS
1. *Guac Dip Rocks the House*
2. *Happy Housewarming*
3. *Friends Make a House a Home*
4. *Celebrating Our New Home*
5. *The Big Move*

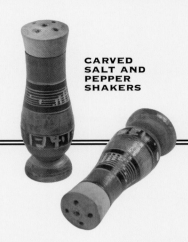

CARVED SALT AND PEPPER SHAKERS

cut out. Use the pattern to cut the hat from red paper. Embellish with stickers.

4 Print recipe on a decorative background as desired, using the photo as a guide.

5 Cut 12-inch-long pieces of fiber and ribbon.

Drape approximately a dozen strands of fiber and one ribbon across the top of each yellow print background paper. Hold the fibers in place by adhering guitar and maraca stickers at each corner.

6 Press the sticker headline on the left-hand page, centered below the fibers. Adhere the remaining elements in place.

DEFINE THE SOMBRERO WITH STICKERS.

GUACAMOLE

MASH 2 PITTED AND PEELED AVOCADOS WITH FORK. STIR IN 1 TBSP. GRATED ONION, 1 TBSP. LEMON JUICE, 1 TSP. SALT, AND 1/4 TSP. CHILI POWDER. SPREAD 1/3 C. MAYONNAISE OVER MIXTURE, SEALING TO EDGES OF BOWL. CHILL. AT SERVING TIME, BLEND MAYONNAISE INTO MIXTURE. SERVE WITH CORN CHIPS.

TRIM THE TOP OF THE MOUNTING PAPER WITH DECORATIVE-EDGE SCISSORS.

B.Y.O.L.—BRING YOUR OWN LOBSTER

Let the colors and theme of a party invitation lead the way to a super scrapbook entry.

WHAT YOU NEED

Recipe; photos; party invitation

Two 12-inch squares of red-and-green plaid scrapbook paper

Two 10-inch squares of royal blue card stock

Card stock in bright blue, periwinkle blue, red, yellow, green, and white

Tracing paper

Red crafting foam

Two ¼-inch flat black buttons

2 small wiggly eyes

Nylon twine; computer and printer

Scissors; paper cutter

Lettering template

Pencil; ruler

Blue marking pen

Adhesive

WHAT TO DO

1 Crop the photos and mount on bright papers. Trim ⅛ inch beyond the edges of the photos.

2 Trace and cut out the lobster pattern, *page 107.*

A TEMPLATE AIDS IN CONSISTENT LETTERING.

INCLUDE A PARTY INVITATION TO SET THE TONE AND AS INSTANT JOURNALING.

PICNIC DISHES, CIRCA 1970

Trace around the pattern shapes on red foam; cut out.

3 Print the recipe from a computer. Crop and mount to blue card stock. Trim ⅛ inch beyond the edge of the recipe.

4 Using a lettering template, write a headline on yellow paper using a blue marking pen. Leave enough space between words to crop each one separately, cutting with wavy lines.

5 Using the photos as guides, adhere pieces in place. Glue buttons on lobster for eyes. Glue a wiggly eye on each button.

6 Cut four 9-inch lengths of twine. Knot each piece 1 inch from the ends; glue to top and bottom of each page.

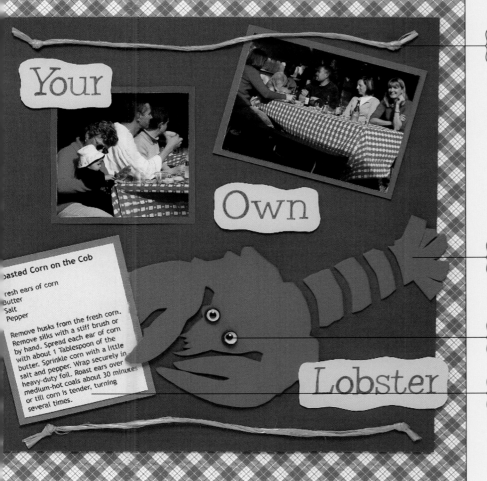

ATTACH PIECES OF TWINE AS PAGE BORDERS.

USE CRAFTING FOAM TO CREATE A DIMENSIONAL LOBSTER.

MOUNT WIGGLY EYES ON BUTTONS FOR EMPHASIS.

POSITION THE RECIPE TO LOOK AS THOUGH THE LOBSTER IS HOLDING IT.

Roasted Corn on the Cob

fresh ears of corn
Butter
Salt
Pepper

Remove husks from the fresh corn. Remove silks with a stiff brush or by hand. Spread each ear of corn with about 1 Tablespoon of the butter. Sprinkle corn with a little salt and pepper. Wrap securely in heavy-duty foil. Roast ears over medium-hot coals about 30 minutes or till corn is tender, turning several times.

USE A PURCHASED PHOTO STRIP FOR IMPACT.

TRACE A DIE CUT TO MAKE FOOTBALL PLAYER.

DRAW YARDAGE LINES USING WHITE ARTIST'S PASTEL.

CUT A WHITE STICKER TO DETAIL FOOTBALL.

USE A CORNER ROUNDER TO SOFTEN EDGES.

SUPER BOWL

No matter who wins the big game, these pages hold champion rankings.

WHAT YOU NEED

Recipe; photos

3×5-inch Super Bowl art

Two 12-inch squares of sky print paper; grass print paper; card stock in light blue, yellow, brown, white, and black

Football photo strip (available in scrapbooking stores)

Tracing paper; football player die cut; stickers, 1×3-inch white and football-theme

Computer and printer; scissors; paper cutter

Corner rounder; pencil; ruler

White artist's pastel; hair spray

Black marking pen; adhesive

WHAT TO DO

1 Crop the photos and round the corners. Mount photos on light blue paper. Trim 1/8-inch narrow borders.

2 Trace the patterns, *page 108*, and cut out. Trace around football on brown, football details on white stickers, and goalpost on yellow. Trace around the football player die cut on brown. Cut out pieces. Cut one additional post in reverse.

3 Print the recipe. Crop and mount on the Super Bowl art piece.

4 Cut two 3¼-inch-wide strips from grass paper. Adhere one strip to each sky background. Use artist's pastel to draw yardage lines. Mist with hair spray to keep pastel from smudging.

5 Using photo as a guide, adhere pieces in place, starting with the football photo strip on the left-hand page. Press football-theme stickers around recipe.

6 Write the journaling below photos.

HAPPY THANKSGIVING

Gathering together to give thanks for family, friends, and favorite dishes is the theme of this leaf-laden design.

WHAT YOU NEED

Recipe; photos
12-inch squares of mottled orange and green leaf papers
Two 12-inch squares of white leaf-print paper
Apple recipe card
Turkey die cut
Paper leaves
Plaid sticker border
Brown alphabet stickers
Autumn-theme stickers
Paper cutter
Corner rounder; ruler
Brown fine-line marking pen
Adhesive

WHAT TO DO

1 Trim the photos and use a corner rounder on the corners. Mount the photos on green leaf paper, trimming ⅛ inch beyond photos and rounding corners. Mount photos for left page on white leaf-print paper; trim ⅛-inch borders.

2 For grass, cut a rounded 12-inch-long strip from green leaf paper. Adhere to lower edge of mottled orange paper.

3 Adhere plaid sticker borders at the top and bottom of each page. Adhere photos in place.

4 Use a brown marking pen to write recipe on apple card. Adhere in place.

5 Adhere leaves, stickers, and die cut.

USE A DECORATIVE CARD TO RECORD RECIPE ON.

MAKE AN ATTRACTIVE BORDER USING STICKER STRIPS.

USE A CORNER ROUNDER FOR CROPPING.

EMBELLISH THE PAGES WITH REALISTIC-LOOKING PAPER LEAVES.

USE A TURKEY DIE CUT TO SET THE THEME.

PUMPKIN CARVIN' PARTY

Cut out foam pumpkins to adorn pages boasting spook-tacular Halloween traditions.

WHAT YOU NEED

Recipe; photos
12-inch squares of swirled metallic paper in copper and gold
12-inch-long paper zigzag borders in green and dark red scribble prints
Dark red scribble print paper
Dark orange rice paper
White printer paper
Tracing paper
Orange crafting foam
Pipe cleaners in brown and green
Paper cutter
Circle cutter
Oval cutter
Ice pick
Scissors; pencil
Computer and printer
Thick white crafts glue
Adhesive

WHAT TO DO

1 Trim the photos and mount on dark orange rice paper; trim ⅛ inch beyond photos.

2 Trace pumpkin patterns, *page 106,* and cut out shapes. Use pattern pieces to

PRINT HEADLINE ON BORDER PAPER FOR CONTINUITY.

USE BORDERS ALL AROUND TO FRAME THE SPREAD.

LAYER FOAM PIECES TO MAKE PUMPKINS; ADD PIPE CLEANER STEMS AND VINES.

HALLOWEEN COOKIE CUTTERS, CIRCA 1960

cut two pumpkins of each size from foam. Adhere the layers together using crafts glue.

3 Adhere zigzag borders to the top, bottom, and outer edges, placing dark red on the gold background and green on the copper.

4 Print the headline on red scribble paper and the recipe on white paper. Crop around word grouping. Crop the recipe and mount on rice paper; trim a ⅛-inch border.

5 Adhere pieces in place. To make pumpkin stems,

cut 1½-inch pieces of brown pipe cleaners; fold in half. For vines, cut 2-inch-long pieces of green pipe cleaners and wrap around an ice pick. Glue a stem and vine to the top of each pumpkin.

USE CONTRASTING BACKGROUND AND BORDER COLORS FOR EACH PAGE TO ADD INTEREST.

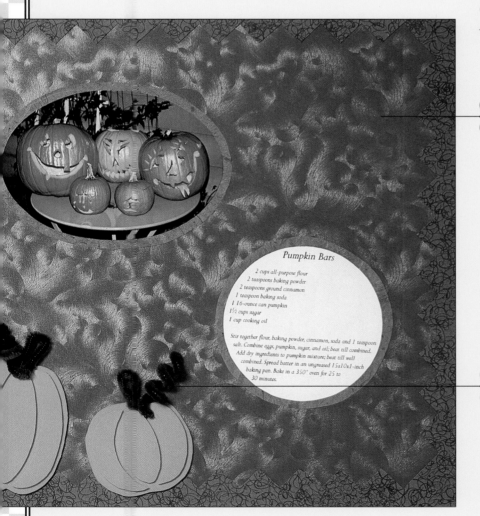

Pumpkin Bars

2 cups all-purpose flour
2 teaspoons baking powder
2 teaspoons ground cinnamon
1 teaspoon baking soda
1 16-ounce can pumpkin
1½ cups sugar
1 cup cooking oil

Stir together flour, baking powder, cinnamon, soda and 1 teaspoon salt. Combine eggs, pumpkin, sugar, and oil; beat till combined. Add dry ingredients to pumpkin mixture; beat till well combined. Spread batter in an ungreased 15x10x1-inch baking pan. Bake in a 350° oven for 25 to 30 minutes.

WRAP PIPE CLEANERS AROUND AN ICE PICK TO SHAPE INTO SPIRALS.

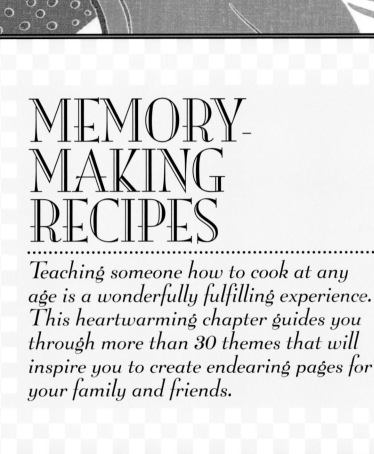

MEMORY-MAKING RECIPES

Teaching someone how to cook at any age is a wonderfully fulfilling experience. This heartwarming chapter guides you through more than 30 themes that will inspire you to create endearing pages for your family and friends.

COOKIE HOUSES

For such baked specialties as cookie houses, this idea takes the cake!

WHAT YOU NEED

Photos
Two 8½×11-inch rectangles of
  green card stock
8½×11-inch rectangles of dark
  green card stock
Two 8½×11-inch beige card stock
Small eyelets
Paper cutter
Crafts knife; corner rounder
Eyelet tool
Brown chalk
Computer and printer
Fine-line brown marking pen
Adhesive foam mounts, such as
  Pop Dots
Adhesive

WHAT TO DO

1 Crop the photos and use a
corner rounder on each.
Mount on beige card stock and
trim narrow borders.

2 From dark green card
stock, use a paper cutter
to cut one 1×8½-inch strip and
two ½×8½-inch strips. Adhere
the strips in place.

USE EYELETS FOR INTEREST.

COMPUTER-GENERATE A
HEADLINE TO COORDINATE
WITH PAPER COLORS.

USE A CORNER
ROUNDER ON PHOTOS AND
MOUNTING PAPER.

Cookie Houses, Easter 1994

In my mom's family
is a tradition of making
cookie houses at Easter.
Using the recipe on the
vious page and mom's
terns, we made these c
cottages, complete wit
and a gumdrop tree

Chimney

Chimney
part

Bailey makes cookies, Christmas 1994

BUTTER BOX, CIRCA 1940

3 Generate the headline on a computer and print in green, with a lighter green shadow if desired. Trim to a ¾×7½-inch strip. Insert an eyelet at each end. Use mounts to adhere the headline to the background strip.

4 Cut cookie house shapes from beige card stock. Chalk the edges. Hand-draw dashed lines around the edges and openings using a brown marking pen. Label each piece.

5 Glue photos and house pieces in place.

6 Cut four ¾-inch squares from dark green. Insert an eyelet in each. Adhere the squares to the background using adhesive mounts.

side

roof

side

{ CHALK THE EDGES FOR A VINTAGE LOOK.

{ MAKE DASHED LINES WITH A MARKING PEN.

{ TO ADD DIMENSION, MOUNT SOME OF THE PIECES USING ADHESIVE MOUNTS.

STATE FAIR CAKE

When cooks of the family enter the state fair, honor their entries with a winning scrapbook page.

WHAT YOU NEED

Recipe

Photos

Two 8½×11-inch green plaid papers

Card stock in off-white, green, and black

Farm animal stickers

Paper cutter

Fine-line marking pens in black and dark green

Black calligraphy pen

Adhesive

WHAT TO DO

1 Crop photos and recipe and mount on card stock that contrasts with background.

2 Handwrite journaling using a green marking pen on off-white card stock. Use a calligraphy pen to write the

USE A CALLIGRAPHY PEN TO HANDWRITE THE HEADLINE.

1 package 2-layer-size regular yellow cake mix or white cake mix

1 4-serving-size package instant vanilla pudding mix

2 beaten eggs

1 8-ounce carton dairy sour cream

¾ cup milk

¼ cup cooking oil

¼ cup sugar

~~¼ cup chopped nuts~~

1 teaspoon ground cinnamon

1 teaspoon ~~unsweetened cocoa~~ powder

Sifted powdered sugar or powdered sugar glaze

1. Grease and flour a 10-inch fluted tube pan. Set aside.

2. In a large mixing bowl, combine the dry cake and pudding mixes. Add eggs, sour cream, milk and cooking oil, ~~stirring till~~ batter is almost smooth.

3. In a small bowl, combine the sugar, nuts, cinnamon and cocoa powder.

4. Pour *half of the cake batter* into the prepared pan. Top with the nut mixture. Top with remaining batter.

5. Bake in a 325° oven for 55 to 60 minutes or till a toothpick inserted near the center comes out clean. Let cool in pan on a wire rack for 10 minutes. Remove from pan and cool completely on

a wire rack. Sprinkle with sifted powdered sugar or drizzle with a powdered sugar glaze. Makes 12 servings.

From Midwest Living magazine

PHOTOCOPY A RECIPE, COMPLETE WITH HANDWRITTEN SCRIBBLES.

MOUNT PHOTOS ON OFF-WHITE TO SEPARATE FROM BACKGROUND.

HEADLINE IDEAS

1. *It Doesn't Matter Whether You Win, It's How You Bake the Cake*
2. *You're a Prize in My Eyes*
3. *The Cake That Took Honors*
4. *A Winner of a Cake*

MILK BOTTLES, CIRCA 1940

headline. Use a fine black marking pen to dot around letters in headline and headline and journaling blocks with long dashed lines. Mount headline to dark green card stock and trim an even border all around.

3 Place stickers on a green card stock rectangle. Trim to fit layout.

4 Arrange pieces, aligning edges for a neat appearance. Adhere in place.

the past several years, m_ mom _ made this cake and taken it in camper to the Iowa State Fair. _ce this is the only time of y_ar she _kes it, we now call it "State Fair _ke." As a child, I camped at t_e fair _h year and now my parents _re _mping with our daughter, B_iley. _ have many fond memories o_ the _! Bailey is pictured with m_ _ents & other friends, 1996 & 1999.

USE THEMED PHOTOS ALONG WITH THE RECIPE WHEN A PHOTO OF THE BAKED ITEM IS UNAVAILABLE.

OUTLINE HEADLINE AND JOURNAL BOXES WITH HAND-DRAWN DASHED LINES.

CHOOSE STICKERS TO CARRY OUT A THEME.

FOR MY SWEET ANGEL—HER LITTLE BOOK

When kids like to help in the kitchen with everything from cracking eggs to stirring up batter, memories are being made. Capture those precious moments to reflect upon as your little angels grow.

WHAT YOU NEED FOR THE BOOK

Recipes; photos
5½×7¼-inch rectangles of card stock in coordinating colors (or size to fit scrapbook sleeves)
Vellum; fibers; brown chalk
Round brads; round eyelets
Stickers; die cuts; eyelet tool
Computer and printer
Paper cutter; scissors
Paper punches; fine-line black marking pen; adhesive

SEPARATE DARK PHOTOS FROM DARK BACKGROUNDS BY MOUNTING ON WHITE.

CUT MOTIFS FROM PRINT BACKGROUND PAPER FOR STICKERLIKE ACCENTS.

CHOOSE PAPERS WITH MOTIFS THE CHILD LIKES.

USE A PURCHASED DIE CUT FOR A WHIMSICAL TOUCH.

LET THE CHILD TYPE THE RECIPE, THEN RECORD THAT FACT IN THE JOURNALING.

ADD A COMPUTER-GENERATED BORDER TO PRINTED JOURNALING.

WAFERS

"Ingredients:
Wafers,
Frosting,
That's about
it!"

"How to make them :
First you take Two Wafers &
put frosting on both of them
& stick them together & you
eat them.

THAT'S ALL!"

"Here's a really good snack for pre-schoolers (and grown-ups, too)!" Bailey was so proud that she typed this recipe!
Bailey - 1996 - Age 3

USE FIBERS TO MAKE RULES AROUND PAGES.

COMBINE PAPERS TO BREAK UP BACKGROUND.

PRINT RECIPE IN HOLIDAY COLORS TO CARRY OUT THE THEME.

EMBELLISH A DIE CUT WITH BRADS AND CHALK FOR ADDED INTEREST.

TEAR MOUNTING PAPER TO CREATE A RAGGED EDGE.

OVERLAP MAT AND PHOTO WITH MOTIFS CUT FROM BACKGROUND PAPERS.

MAGIC REINDEER FOOD

- Glitter
- Wooden spoon
- Oats
- Big bowl
- Small bags

Making It:
Pour oats into big bowl.
Pour glitter into big bowl.
Stir. One teaspoon per bag.

On Christmas Eve, sprinkle this magic reindeer food on your lawn. The sparkling glitter in the moonlight and sweet smell of oats will attract Rudolph to your house!

This tasty recipe was given to us by Dawn Johnson. Over the years, Bailey has mixed up large quantities for friends and family. Every Christmas Eve, she sprinkles a bit on the lawn. Rudolph has never missed our house!
Bailey – December 1997 – Age 4

WHAT TO DO

1 When choosing papers for a mini scrapbook with several diverse themes, devote a spread to each subject and choose fitting papers. Notice on these sample scrapbook pages, *pages 70–77,* that papers vary for each subject. The headline is used because a mom created this book for her young daughter. You can change it to fit your mini book.

2 Crop the photos as desired. Single- or double-mount the photos on card stock, tearing the edges of mounting paper or cutting it clean.

3 To create the backgrounds, cut or tear papers and adhere in place using the photos for inspiration. Read the callouts by each page to note how to create each of the special effects.

continued on page 72

FOR MY SWEET ANGEL BOOK
continued

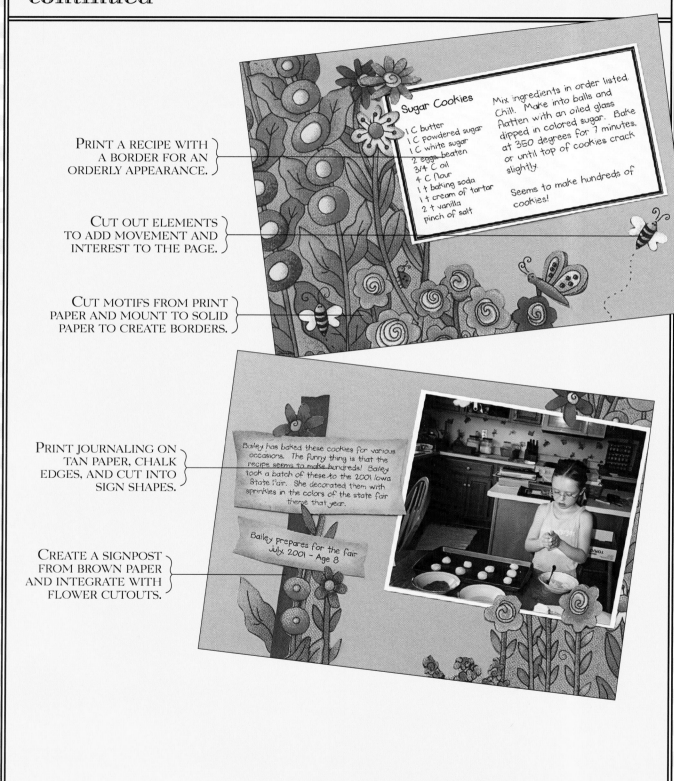

PRINT A RECIPE WITH
A BORDER FOR AN
ORDERLY APPEARANCE.

CUT OUT ELEMENTS
TO ADD MOVEMENT AND
INTEREST TO THE PAGE.

CUT MOTIFS FROM PRINT
PAPER AND MOUNT TO SOLID
PAPER TO CREATE BORDERS.

PRINT JOURNALING ON
TAN PAPER, CHALK
EDGES, AND CUT INTO
SIGN SHAPES.

CREATE A SIGNPOST
FROM BROWN PAPER
AND INTEGRATE WITH
FLOWER CUTOUTS.

Sugar Cookies

1 C butter
1 C powdered sugar
1 C white sugar
2 eggs, beaten
3/4 C oil
4 C flour
1 t baking soda
1 t cream of tartar
2 t vanilla
pinch of salt

Mix ingredients in order listed. Chill. Make into balls and flatten with an oiled glass dipped in colored sugar. Bake at 350 degrees for 7 minutes, or until top of cookies crack slightly.

Seems to make hundreds of cookies!

Bailey has baked these cookies for various occasions. The funny thing is that the recipe seems to make hundreds! Bailey took a batch of these to the 2001 Iowa State Fair. She decorated them with sprinkles in the colors of the state fair theme that year.

Bailey prepares for the fair
July 2001 - Age 8

COOKIE CUTTERS,
CIRCA 1950

POLKA DOT BOWL,
CIRCA 1950

Extra Tall & Sprinkly Rice Krispy Treats

TRIM MOUNTING
PAPERS WITH
SLIGHTLY IRREGULAR
CUTS FOR A BREAK
FROM STRAIGHT
CUTS.

TAKE PHOTOS OF THE
CHILD'S CREATIONS IN
THE KITCHEN.

THESE PAPERS
ENHANCE THE STATE
FAIR THEME.

ADD A BORDER AROUND A
RECIPE THAT RELATES TO THE
THEME OF THE PAGE.

INCLUDE A RIBBON
SILHOUETTE FROM A PHOTO
OR PHOTOCOPY.

USE EYELETS TO HOLD
JOURNALING IN PLACE.

Extra Tall & Sprinkly Rice Krispy Treats

- 5 cups Rice Krispies
- 1/4 cup margarine
- 4 cups mini marshmallows or (40) large marshmallows
- Colored sprinkles

Melt margarine. Add marshmallows. Stir continuously until melted. Stir in Rice Krispies. Spread into greased 9 x 9 x 2 pan with greased hands. Press down hard with the flat bottom of a glass. Rice Krispy Treats will be extra tall and firmly packed. Decorate with colored sprinkles. Let set, then cut into squares.

August, 2001 - Bailey, age 8
Bailey entered her "Extra Tall & Sprinkly Rice Krispy Treats" in the 2001 Iowa State Fair. She decided to use the original recipe but compress it down into the a smaller than recommended pan. This created an "extra tall" treat. The sprinkles added a festive touch. Judges liked the taste and the name of her treats and awarded her first prize, as shown in this photo.

continued on page 74

FOR MY SWEET ANGEL BOOK
continued

ATTACH TINY DIE CUTS OR
STICKERS TO ADD PLAYFUL
TOUCHES.

PRINT A HEADLINE ON
COLORED VELLUM TO CREATE
THE LOOK OF PLAID.

PRINT JOURNALING ON
PHOTO-MOUNTING PAPER
FOR ORGANIZATION.

APPLY STICKERS
TO PAPERS FOR SMALL
FRAMED PICTURES.

ADHERE ADDITIONAL
PAPER STRIP ON
STRIPE PAPER FOR A
DIMENSIONAL LOOK.

Merry-Go-Round Cake

Bailey in the camper preparing for her presentation
August 2001 – Age 8

Bailey entered the "Beyond Macaroni and Cheese" competition at the 2001 Iowa State Fair. Kids and moms were to work together to make a recipe in front of judges and an audience. Bailey made a Merry-Go-Round cake, a double layer cake which she had made from scratch several times. At the fair, Bailey did an great job of narrating the whole process, mixing up the ingredients and assembling the cake. Mom's only job was holding the bowl. The judges couldn't believe how an 8-year-old girl could make such a complicated recipe and describe it so well. Bailey won a blue ribbon for her efforts!

Bake-a-Cake

Margarine (for greasing cake pans)
2 1/2 C sifted cake flour
4 t baking powder
1/2 t salt
1 1/4 C sugar
2 eggs
3/4 cup margarine, softened
3/4 C milk
1 t vanilla extract
1 heaping T margarine

Preheat oven to 350 degrees. Grease 2 9-inch round pans with margarine. Mix the flour, baking powder, salt and sugar together, then sift them into a bowl. Break the eggs into a large bowl. Add margarine, milk, vanilla, and mayonnaise and beat with spoon until light and fluffy. Mix the flour mixture into the egg mixture a little at a time, then beat with a mixer until the batter is creamy. Pour batter into cake pans. Bake for 20-25 minutes. Cool for 5 minutes then circle a knife around the edges and turn them upside down onto a wire rack to finish cooling.

Merry-Go-Round Cake

2 9-inch cake layers
Frosting
Colored paper
Plastic straws
24 animal crackers

Place 1 cake layer on a plate. Spread with some of the frosting, then put the other cake layer on top. Frost the side and top of the cake with the rest of the frosting. Place a 10-inch dinner plate face down on the piece of colored paper. Tracy around the edge with a pencil then cut out the circle. Make 6 pencil marks equally spaced around the circle about 3/4 inch away from the edge. Poke a hole in each of the marks. Push out the top. With the paper attached, stick the straws through the holes until 1 inch comes longer sides of the straws into the cake. Stand 4 animal crackers in a circle around each straw.

HEADLINE IDEAS

1. *Baking with Granny*
2. *Me and Grandma Make Treats*
3. *In the Kitchen with Nana*
4. *I Love to Make Candy!*
5. *Candy is MY Kind of Food!*

ANIMAL COOKIE CUTTERS, CIRCA 1950

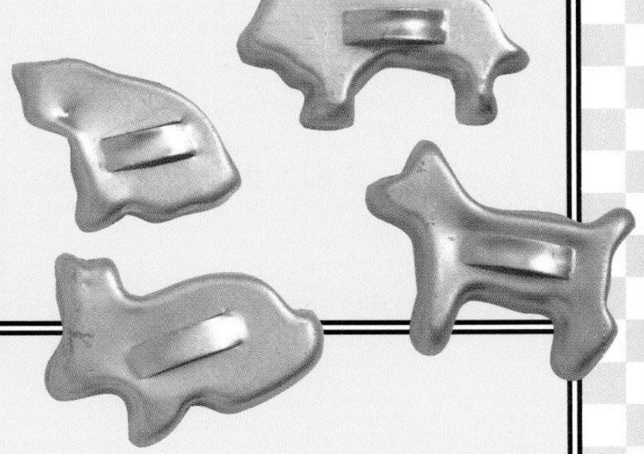

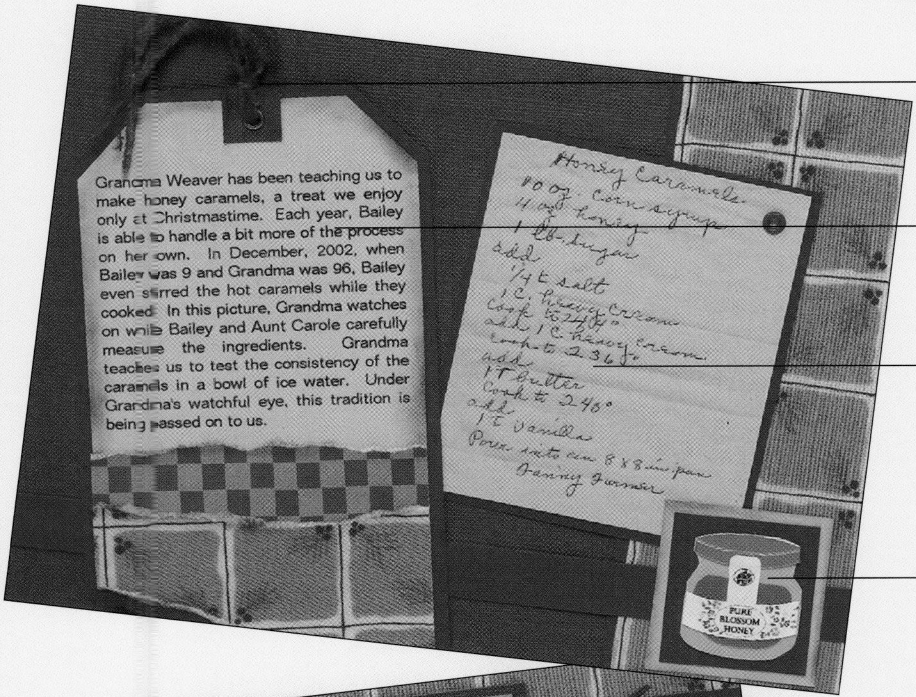

Grandma Weaver has been teaching us to make honey caramels, a treat we enjoy only at Christmastime. Each year, Bailey is able to handle a bit more of the process on her own. In December, 2002, when Bailey was 9 and Grandma was 96, Bailey even stirred the hot caramels while they cooked. In this picture, Grandma watches on while Bailey and Aunt Carole carefully measure the ingredients. Grandma teaches us to test the consistency of the caramels in a bowl of ice water. Under Grandma's watchful eye, this tradition is being passed on to us.
Honey Caramels
PURE BLOSSOM HONEY

ATTACH FIBER THROUGH THE TAG EYELET.

CUT PAPER IN A TAG SHAPE AND INSERT AN EYELET AT THE TOP.

PHOTOCOPY A HANDWRITTEN RECIPE ON CREAM-COLOR PAPER FOR AN AUTHENTIC LOOK.

AFFIX A STICKER THAT EMPHASIZES A RECIPE INGREDIENT.

Honey Caramels

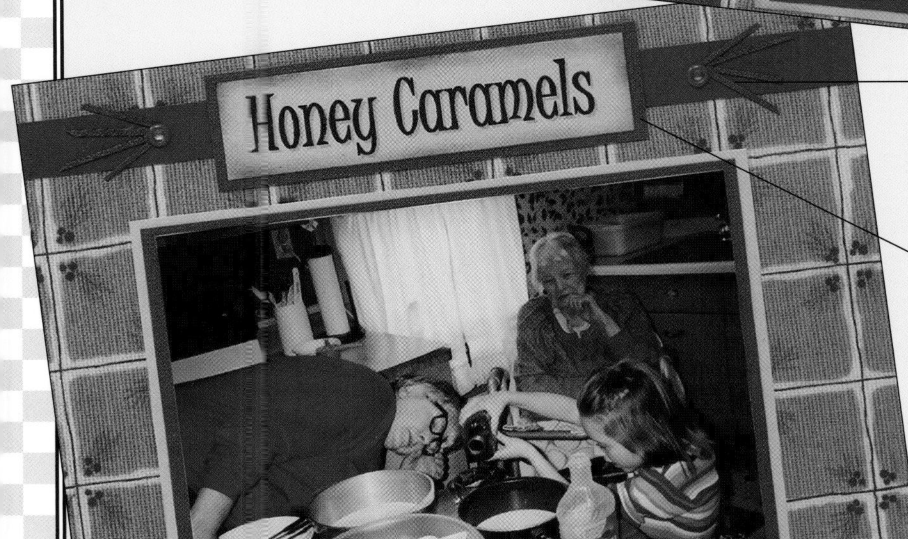

APPLY PAPER STRIPS NEXT TO EYELETS FOR AN EVERGREEN AND BERRY EFFECT.

CHALK THE EDGES OF A COMPUTER-GENERATED HEADLINE FOR VINTAGE APPEAL.

continued on page 72

ADHERE TINY PAPER
TRIANGLES IN THEME
COLORS TO ACCENT
THE BORDER STRIP.

Bailey entered these
Haunted Halloween Hats
in the 2002 Iowa State Fair
"Trick-or-Treat Treats"
Junior Food Division. She
was excited to win third
prize in this category!
Bailey is shown here
creating the prize-winning
treats to take to the fair.

Bailey – August, 2002 – Age 9

USE DIE CUTS OR STICKERS
TO REINFORCE THE THEME
OF THE PAGE.

INSERT BRADS IN
COLORS THAT GO ALONG
WITH THE TOPIC.

CREATE HEADLINE AND
RECIPE TOGETHER FOR
EXPEDIENCY.

SILHOUETTE A
PART OF THE PHOTO
FOR IMPACT.

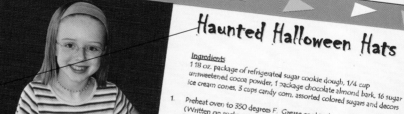

Haunted Halloween Hats

Ingredients

1 18 oz. package of refrigerated sugar cookie dough, 1/4 cup unsweetened cocoa powder, 1 package chocolate almond bark, 16 sugar ice cream cones, 3 cups candy corn, assorted colored sugars and decors

1. Preheat oven to 350 degrees F. Grease cookie sheets if needed. (Written on package instructions.) Mix dough and cocoa powder in large bowl until blended well. Divide dough into 16 pieces, and then shape into balls. Flatten each ball on prepared cookie sheets into 3 1/2 to 4 inch circles. Bake for about 5 min., depending on thickness of cookies. Cool on wire racks.

2. Line large tray with waxed paper. Melt almond bark in microwave according to package instructions, reserving 2 small portions. Coat sugar cones with chocolate, using a clean pastry brush. Stand up on tray, then freeze for 15 minutes, or until chocolate is completely hardened.

3. Melt remaining almond bark in microwave.

4. Fill cones with candy corn, and then brush the cone edge with melted chocolate. Place cookie on cone. Decorate as desired with colored sugars, decors, and melted chocolate.

Makes 16 servings.

JELLO MOLDS,
CIRCA 1950

COCOA TIN,
CIRCA 1910

The Big Bad Wolf's Brownies

- Margarine (for greasing pan)
- 1 stick margarine
- 2 squares (2 ounces) semi-sweet chocolate
- 1 cup sugar
- 1/2 cup unsifted flour
- 1 t baking powder
- 1 t vanilla extract
- 2 eggs, lightly beaten

Preheat oven to 350 degrees. Grease a 9x9x2-inch baking pan with margarine. Melt margarine and chocolate in microwave (1.5 minutes). Stir in sugar, flour, baking powder, vanilla, and eggs. Beat well. Pour into baking pan. Bake for 42 minutes. Cool on rack and cut brownies into squares. Makes 16.

ATTACH A BRAD TO
LOOK LIKE A BERRY.

The Big Bad Wolf's Brownies

EMBELLISH A
COMPUTER-GENERATED
HEADLINE WITH TREE
PUNCHED PIECES
AND CUTOUTS FROM
PRINTED PAPER.

CHALK THE EDGES OF
TORN PAPER FOR A
BACKGROUND ACCENT.

CUT PAPER IN A TAG SHAPE
FOR ADDED INTEREST.

Bailey found this recipe for from-scratch brownies in her Mickey Mouse cookbook. She insists on doing most of her baking from scratch. These brownies are quite tasty, especially sprinkled with powdered sugar. She took a batch of these brownies to the 2001 Iowa State Fair. In this picture, she is sampling a test batch, one of the benefits of entering fair competitions!

DECORATE TAG WITH
CHALKED PRINTED PAPER.

DILL-ICIOUS PICKLES

When a father and son team up to carry on a family tradition in the kitchen, capture the moment on film.

WHAT YOU NEED

Recipe; photos
12-inch square of medium green card stock
11 1/2-inch square of check green paper
Card stock in dark and light green
Corner rounder
Computer and printer
Scissors; ruler
Paper cutter
Adhesive foam mounts, such as Pop Dots
Adhesive

WHAT TO DO

1 Crop the photos, rounding the corners or silhouetting the images. Mount the photos on dark green card stock. Along the top and sides, trim 1/8 inch beyond each photo; leave 3/4 inch at the bottom, cutting a straight edge.

2 Print the journaling, captions, headline, and recipe on light green card stock.

Trim the photo captions to fit below the photos. Mount the journaling and recipe on dark green and trim 1/8 inch beyond light green paper edges.

3 To give some of the silhouetted pieces dimension, mount them on adhesive mounts. Arrange the elements and adhere in place.

Family Pickle History

When Kellie was growing up, they called her great grandparents "Grandma & Grandpa Dill Pickle" because Grandpa canned pickles. Their real names were Bill & Tillie Behle.

Grandpa had crocks with pickle brine & cucumbers brewing in his garage. Jars filled his cellar basement. A meal wasn't complete without a pickle. And whenever he visited, he always brought a jar.

Although Nathan never met Grandpa Dill Pickle, he & Doug thought they would carry on the family tradition and brew their own pickles. They grew the cucumbers & dill in the garden, canned one batch, and had good results.

Nathan & Doug proudly show off their 1st jar of pickles.

1995

Grandpa's Dill Pickles

Cucumbers
(unpeeled and with a bit of the stem, if possible)
2 heads of dill
Fresh Grape Leaves
3/4 cup cider vinegar
1 1/2 tablespoons canning salt
1 clove garlic, peeled and sliced

Place half the dill & a grape leaf at the bottom of a sterilized, self-sealing quart jar and then pack the jar with cucumbers. Add vinegar, canning salt, garlic, and enough cold water to cover the cukes. Lay the rest of the dill on top of the mixture and tightly screw on the lid. Set the jar in a canner filled with water, making sure the water covers the jars. Bring to a gentle boil and let boil for 5-10 minutes. Turn off the heat. When the jar is cool enough to handle, remove it from the pan. Refrigerate; the pickles will be ready to eat in 3 weeks and should be eaten within a year.

Doug's surprised response: "They're actually GOOD!"

Nathan takes the first Bite and likes them.

OUTLINE THE JOURNAL BOX FOR A POLISHED LOOK.

CAPITALIZE WORD FOR IMPACT.

SILHOUETTE SHAPES AND ADHERE A FEW USING MOUNTS FOR DIMENSION.

ROUND THE CORNERS AT THE TOP AND CUT A STRAIGHT EDGE ALONG THE BOTTOM.

PLACE A PHOTO CAPTION ON THE MOUNTING PAPER TO MAKE A UNIT.

WEAVE THE CORNERS OF PAPER
STRIPS FOR A TEXTURED MAT.

STAMP PART OF THE
HEADLINE LETTERING.

TIE TWINE THROUGH BUTTONS FOR
A SEWN-ON APPEARANCE.

WEAVE PAPER STRIPS FOR AN
INTERESTING FRAME.

USE DIMENSIONAL
STICKERS TO
ACCENT THE
BAKING THEME.

WHAT'S COOKIN'?

Even when home cookin' starts with a mix, these three girls have earned the right to be proud bakers!

WHAT YOU NEED

Photos

Two 12-inch pieces of red
card stock

Coordinating papers and
rubber stamps and ink, such as
Club Scrap's Mocha Java Kit

Dimensional stickers with a
baking theme

Three ½-inch buttons

Twine

Computer and printer

Scissors

Paper cutter

Thick white crafts glue

Adhesive

WHAT TO DO

1 Crop the photos and mount on contrasting paper. For a woven border, cut eight paper strips and adhere around the mat, weaving the corners together.

2 For woven paper squares, cut paper strips and weave together. Mount on paper; double-mount if desired.

3 Computer-generate journaling and print on light-color coordinating paper. Trim as desired.

4 For the headline, stamp two circular shapes for the Os. Write or computer-generate WHAT'S and the remaining letters.

5 Adhere the pieces in place, applying a dimensional sticker in the center of each woven square.

6 Knot twine through each button and glue buttons below the headline.

MONKEY BREAD

When a scrapbook page focuses on this recipe, there's no monkeyin' around!

WOODEN HONEY DIPPER

WHAT YOU NEED

Recipe
Photos
Two 12-inch squares of
  dripping-honey print paper
Brown card stock
Monkey die cut
Brown marking pen
Paper cutter
Computer and printer
Ruler; scissors; adhesive

WHAT TO DO

1 Crop photos and mount on brown card stock. Trim ⅛-inch borders.

2 Print recipe and journaling on honey-print paper. Crop around lettering. Mount the recipe on brown card stock; trim ⅛-inch border. Outline the journal box using a marking pen.

3 Print the headline in large letters and use as a pattern to cut letters from background paper.

4 Adhere the pieces to the background honey-print paper, placing the monkey die cut to swing from the Y.

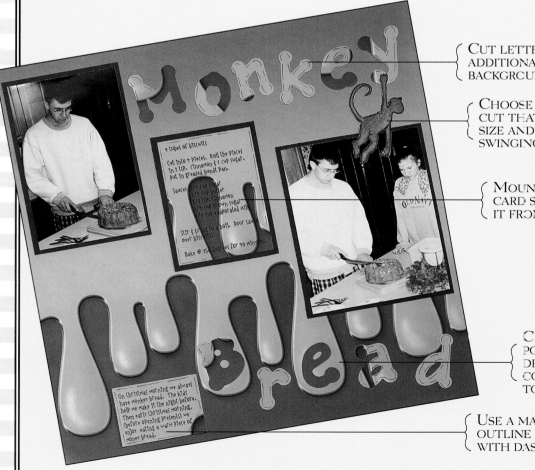

CUT LETTERS FROM ADDITIONAL SHEET OF BACKGROUND PAPER.

CHOOSE A MONKEY DIE CUT THAT IS THE RIGHT SIZE AND IN THE RIGHT SWINGING POSITION.

MOUNT RECIPE ON BROWN CARD STOCK TO SEPARATE IT FROM THE BACKGROUND.

CHECK LETTER POSITIONING TO DETERMINE WHAT COLOR OF PAPER TO USE.

USE A MARKING PEN TO OUTLINE THE JOURNAL BOX WITH DASHED LINES.

24-HOUR SALAD

When a recipe has a connection to time, this scrapbook page idea is "hour" favorite.

USE EYELET LETTERS FOR AN INTERESTING HEADLINE TREATMENT.

RECORD THE DATE USING A DATE STAMP.

USE A CLOCK FACE AND HANDS TO DENOTE TIME.

CRUMPLE PAPER FOR INSTANT TEXTURE.

EMPHASIZE WORDS WITH METAL WORD PLATES.

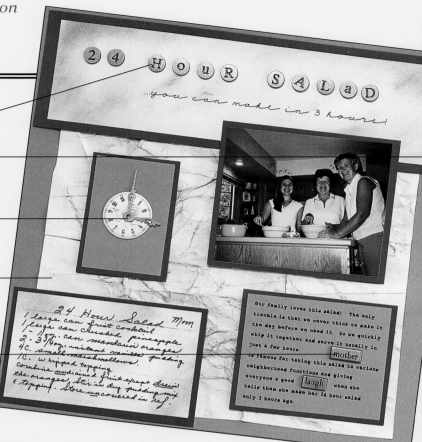

WHAT YOU NEED

Recipe

Photo

12-inch square of light blue card stock

Card stock in light blue, medium blue, and cream

Eyelet letters and words, such as Making Memories

Clock face and hands, such as Jest Charming

Chalks in blue and brown

Date stamp

Ruler

Computer and printer

Paper trimmer

Adhesive

WHAT TO DO

1 Crop the photo and mount on medium blue card stock. Cut a 2¼×3¼-inch rectangle of light blue card stock. Mount to medium blue; trim a ⅛-inch border. Center and adhere the clock face to the layered papers.

2 Print the subhead on cream and the journaling on light blue. For the journaling, leave space to insert metal word plates. Crop the subhead and the journaling and mount each on medium blue; trim a ⅛-inch border. Mount the recipe on medium blue;

trim a ⅛-inch border. Chalk the recipe to give it an aged effect. Stamp the date vertically along the right-hand edge of the subhead.

3 Cut an 11-inch square of cream card stock. Crumple it and reflatten it. Chalk the paper.

4 Center and adhere the crumpled paper to the background card stock. Adhere the remaining elements in place. Use eyelet letters to spell out the headline.

DAD'S BEST GRUB

A tribute to the male cook in the house, this decked-out chef is a delightful accent to a collection of favorite recipes.

WHAT YOU NEED

Recipes

Two 12-inch squares of white card stock

12-inch square of red paper

Papers in black, white, light pink, dark pink, black-and-white check, and red

Tracing paper

1-inch and ¼-inch black adhesive lettering

Pencil; scissors; ruler

Paper cutter

Fine-line black marking pen

Adhesive

WHAT TO DO

1 To make the cook and bowl, trace the patterns, *pages 104 and 109.* Cut out the shapes. Trace around the shapes on corresponding papers. Cut out the pieces. Layer and glue the paper pieces to make the cook and the bowl. Use a pen to write KISS THE COOK on the cook's round red button. Set motifs aside.

2 Cut a 5-inch-wide strip from the 12-inch square of red paper. Glue the 5-inch strip to one sheet of white card stock

USE THE PATTERNS TO CREATE A LAYERED PAPER COOK.

DIAGONALLY CUT BLACK PAPER SQUARES TO CREATE ZIGZAG.

DAD'S BEST GRUB

Potato Corn Casserole

1½ pd. Red River Valley fr. fries
1# Gr. Beef; 1 chopped onion; 1 can cr. style corn; 1 can cream of chicken soup; 1 can cr. of mushroom soup.

Brown beef & onion; add creamed corn & soup
Put fr. fries on bottom of large flat baking dish; Pour over meat mixture and bake 1½ hrs 375° oven - or til potatoes are tender.

**HEAVY DUTY
PAN SCRUBBER,
CIRCA 1910**

and the remaining 7-inch strip to the other sheet. Arrange the pages with the red strips at the outer edges, as shown, *below.*

3 Using a ruler, mark off ten 1-inch squares on black paper. Cut out squares. Cut each square in half diagonally to make 20 triangles. Glue the triangles in rows where red and white papers meet.

4 Glue the paper cook to the wider red paper strip on the left-hand page. Glue the check bowl at a slight angle on the right-hand page.

5 Use large adhesive letters to spell DAD'S BEST GRUB on the left-hand page and YUM, YUM! on the right. Use the small letters to spell a personalized message on the red strip on the right-hand page. Arrange the recipe cards and glue on the page.

6 Cut approximately six small irregular triangles from black paper. Adhere them adjacent to the recipe cards, as shown.

DAD SAYS:
A KISSED COOK
IS A
HAPPY COOK!

yum, yum!

OLD SETTLER'S BAKED BEANS

1# gr. beef)
5 or 6 slices bacon, diced) brown
1 small onion)

1 c. Pork 'n Beans
1 c. Butter Beans (may be drained slightly if there
        is quite a little liquid)
1 c. Kidney Beans

In large casserole mix together: ½ c. br. sugar,
¼ c. catsup, ½ tsp. dry mustard, 2 Tbsp. molasses

Add meat mixture and beans and mix well. Bake at
350° for one hour. Freezes well.

Wild Rice
2 cups raw wild rice
2 cups diced celery
1 cup diced onion
4 slices bacon, crisped & broken
2 cans beef consome or broth
1 can cr. mushroom soup
Cook celery & onion in butter 10 min. covered
Mix with rest of ingred. in flat baking pan.
Let stand 6 - 24 hours. Add water as needed.
Bake 325° 2 1/2 hrs.
Serves 8+

Chicken Enchilada Casserole   Gert
1 med onion chopped or green   7 oz can diced gr. chilies
2 T. butter   1 3# chicken, cooked
2 cans cr. chix soup   boned & diced
1/2 c. water   1 # Monterey Jack cheese
1 doz. corn tortillas   (grated)
                                 sour cream
Saute onion in butter, add soup, chilies & water. Add
diced chicken, salt & pepper. Mix well til all is hot.
In 13x9" dish place a layer of tortillas to cover the
bottom, cut in fourths. On top of first layer put
chicken sauce to cover, then sprinkle with grated
cheese, repeat layers til casserole is filled - ending
with cheese..
Bake 350° oven for 30 minutes - serve with sour
cream on top.

IRREGULAR TRIANGLES ADD
MOVEMENT TO THE PAGE.

ADHESIVE LETTERS MAKE
HEADLINES A SNAP.

PHOTOCOPY ORIGINAL RECIPE
CARDS TO MAINTAIN THE
ORIGINALITY AND PATINA.

FIRST PIZZA

No matter which way you cut it, this pizza page can be assembled quicker than you can say, "Extra cheese, please!"

WHAT YOU NEED

Recipe

Photos

12-inch squares of card stock in black and tan

Cream card stock

12-inch square of pizza-print paper

¾-inch red alphabet stickers

Circle cutter

Scissors; ruler

Black fine-line marking pen

Adhesive

WHAT TO DO

1 Cut a 10-inch-diameter circle from pizza-print paper. For crust, cut a 12-inch-diameter circle from tan card stock, cutting a wavy edge. Cut 1 to 1½ inches inside the outer edge to form a crust. Adhere the crust around the edge of the pizza-print paper. Cut out a wedge from the pizza. Cut a cream wedge to fit the opening. Adhere to the background.

2 Using a circle cutter, crop the photos and mount them on cream card stock. Trim ⅛-inch borders. Adhere photos to pizza-print paper.

3 Use alphabet stickers for a headline.

4 Write a recipe in the wedge using a black marking pen.

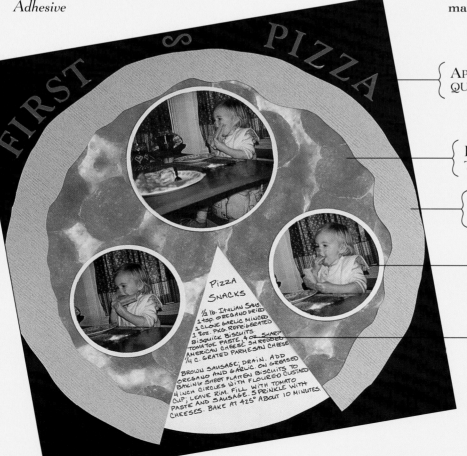

APPLY STICKERS FOR A QUICK HEADLINE.

PIZZA-PRINT PAPER STATES THE THEME AT A GLANCE.

HAND-CUT WAVY LINES TRANSFORM A CIRCLE INTO A CRUST.

CIRCULAR PHOTOS RESEMBLE PEPPERONI SLICES FOR THE PIZZA.

INSERT A WEDGE OF LIGHT-COLOR PAPER TO RECORD THE RECIPE.

DAD'S PASGETTI

Record an adorable toddler moment—when he eats and wears his yummy foods!

HANDWRITE THE RECIPE TO PERSONALIZE IT.

RED PLAID SHOWS UP FROM THE BORDER WITHOUT LOOKING TOO BOLD.

CUT PAPER STRIPS FOR SPAGHETTI.

COMPUTER-GENERATE A HEADLINE IN LARGE LETTERS.

ANGLE THE RECIPE AND PHOTO TO BALANCE THE PAGE AND CREATE MOVEMENT.

WHAT YOU NEED

Recipe

Photo

12-inch red subtle-print card stock

Papers in red plaid, black-and-white polka-dot, yellow stripe, green print, and ivory

Pen with disappearing ink

Black marking pens in fine and medium widths

Computer and printer

Scissors

Paper cutter

Adhesive

WHAT TO DO

1 Crop the photo and mount on red plaid and polka-dot papers.

2 Draw guide lines with disappearing ink for recipe on yellow stripe paper. Write recipe using black marking pens. Trim, leaving approximately ¼ inch around each edge. Mount on polka-dot, plaid, and green print papers, trimming borders.

3 To make the spaghetti, cut 25 approximately ⅛-inch-wide strips from ivory paper.

4 Computer-generate a headline, making large letters with a drop shadow. Print on yellow stripe paper.

5 Adhere the elements in place, starting with the spaghetti. Angle the photo and recipe and trim off two corners of the matting from each.

GERMAN PANCAKES

Let little ones in on the cooking and your time in the kitchen transforms from work to play.

WHAT YOU NEED

Recipe; photos

Two 12-inch squares of light green card stock

Three 1-inch squares of light green card stock

12-inch square of black card stock

Two 8½×11-inch sheets of silver paper

4×8-inch corrugated black paper

2-inch silver alphabet stickers (or smaller depending on headline length)

Computer and printer

Paper cutter; ruler

Silver marking pen

Adhesive

WHAT TO DO

1 Crop the photos and mount on silver paper. Trim ½-inch borders beyond the photo edges.

2 Print the recipe on a computer to fit in a 3¼×7-inch space; print and crop to this size. Adhere recipe to black corrugated paper.

TWO-INCH ALPHABET STICKERS CREATE A BOLD HEADLINE.

HANDWRITE PART OF THE HEADLINE FOR A FUN DESIGN TWIST AND TO SAVE SPACE.

USE CORRUGATED PAPER FOR TEXTURE.

HEADLINE IDEAS

1. *Sunday Morn' Routine*
2. *Laurel and Her Pancakes*
3. *Laurel's Favorite Cakes*
4. *Mommy, Can I Stir?*
5. *Pancakes à la Laurel*

**WOODEN SPOON,
CIRCA 1930**

3 Cut a 4-inch-wide strip from black card stock. Vertically adhere to the edge of one 12-inch sheet of green card stock. Cut two ¼×3-inch-wide strips from silver; adhere along edge of black at the top and bottom of the page.

4 Press lettering in place, personalizing as desired.

(For longer headlines, use smaller alphabet stickers.) Use a silver pen to add to the headline, as on this page for the word GERMAN.

5 Adhere mounted photos in place. Apply a black paper triangle to the right-hand page on the lower right-hand corner of the photo.

6 Cut a 1½×9-inch strip from silver. Cut four ³⁄₈-inch squares from black card stock. Adhere windowpane fashion to top of silver strip. Adhere strip vertically ¼ inch from photo on left page. Adhere mounted recipe over strip.

7 Adhere green paper squares to lower edge of left page, centered on black strip. Press a silver square from letter sticker page in the center of each square.

8 Journal below the photos using a silver marking pen.

PRINT RECENT PHOTOS IN BLACK AND WHITE FOR GRAPHIC IMPACT.

ANCHOR A PHOTO ON THE PAGE WITH A LARGE PAPER PHOTO CORNER.

JACOB & GRANDMA

Even the simplest of recipes can contribute to a classic scrapbook page when seen through the eyes of a child.

WHAT YOU NEED

Recipe
Photos
Two 12-inch squares of light
  yellow card stock
12-inch square of textured blue
  paper
8½×11-inch piece of print
  red paper
Card stock in white and dark blue

Playful animal stickers
  and borders
Computer and printer
Circle cutter
Paper cutter
Decorative-edge scissors
Black marking pen
Adhesive

WHAT TO DO

1 Crop the photos, using a circle cutter for a close-up shot. Mount photos on white card stock and trim ⅛-inch borders. Trim the circular shot with decorative-edge scissors. Mount the circle to blue paper and crop a wide border.

WRITE JOURNALING TO LOOK
LIKE A CHILD'S WRITING.

USE A WIDE PAPER STRIP TO
BALANCE THE PAGE DESIGN.

USE A STICKER BORDER
TO OUTLINE HEADLINE.

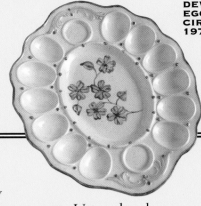
2 Print the headline and recipe, or a child's interpretation of the recipe, on white paper. Trim and mount the recipe on red print paper. Trim ½ inch beyond the edges of the recipe. Write journaling on white paper using a marking pen; mount on red print paper and trim a ⅛-inch border.

3 With decorative-edge scissors, cut two narrow strips from textured blue paper, one long edge straight. Adhere vertically to right page, as shown. With the same decorative-edge scissors, cut a 4½-inch-wide strip from textured blue paper. Adhere vertically to left page, 1 inch from the outer edge.

4 Using the photos as guides, adhere the pieces on the pages. Embellish with animal stickers. To add photo corners, cut small triangles from red print paper. Trim one edge with decorative-edge scissors. Adhere over each photo corner.

5 Write captions using a black marking pen.

How to Make Deviled Eggs
by Jacob Hoogensen

I am going to tell you how to make Deviled Eggs. This is what you need to make it. You need a pan with boiling water and as many ~~raw~~ eggs as you want! First, you put the eggs in boiling water for 1 hour. Then, let them cool. When they are cooled, peel the shells off. Then, cut them open and clear out the inside. Then, mix up the yolk. (You may need to add mayonnaise.) Finally, put the yolk back inside the egg.

Jacob, age 4

PRESS ON PLAYFUL STICKERS FOR A WHIMSICAL TOUCH.

MAKE NOTES OF A RECIPE FROM A CHILD'S POINT OF VIEW.

TRIM WHITE MOUNTING PAPER WITH DECORATIVE-EDGE SCISSORS.

DINER DELIGHTS

You'll feel like putting a quarter in the jukebox when you create this design devoted to '50s style!

WHAT YOU NEED

Recipes

Wallet-size photo

Two 12-inch squares of black card stock

12-inch square of turquoise card stock

8½×11-inch card stock in silver, black, and white

White printer paper

Metallic red fleck alphabet stickers in 1- and 2-inch sizes

Paper cutter

Circle cutter

Computer and printer

½-inch black alphabet stickers

Silver marking pen; ruler

Adhesive

WHAT TO DO

1 To make the record, cut the following circles: a 2-inch circle from 8½×11-inch black card stock, a 3-inch circle from white, a 5¾-inch circle from black, and a 6½-inch circle from silver. Center, layer, and glue circles to make a

METALLIC RED LETTERS ADD '50S FLAIR.

CHOOSE TABLE REMINDERS FROM THE LIST, *BELOW,* FOR A PLAYFUL TOUCH.

SILVER ACCENTS BRING LIFE TO THE PAGE.

USE A CIRCLE CUTTER TO MAKE CUTTING EASY.

TABLE REMINDERS

Clean your plate.

Eat your peas.

Use your napkin.

Thank the cook.

Use your manners.

Chew with your mouth closed.

Elbows off the table.

Use your fork.

What's for dessert?

HEADLINE IDEAS ....

1. *Greg Cooks!*
2. *This College Boy Can Cook*
3. *My College Boy and His Burgers*
4. *Would You Like a Shake with That?*
5. *Greg's Favorite Combo*

ALUMINUM SHERBETS, CIRCA 1950

record shape. Use black alphabet stickers to apply BLUE MOON and 45 on the white layer. Adhere the record to the center of one sheet of black card stock.

2 Press on 2-inch red stickers to spell DINER at the top of page, following the curve of the record. Press on 1-inch red stickers to spell DELIGHTS at the bottom and GOOD EATS on the opposite page, as shown. Use 14 squares from the sticker page (or cut from remaining letters) to make designs between words.

3 Computer-generate recipes and table reminders (see list, *opposite bottom left*) on white paper. Trim recipes approximately ½ inch from copy and trim reminders ⅛ inch from copy, tearing the paper before and after the typing if desired. Mount recipes on turquoise paper and trim narrow borders. Mount a long strip of reminders on a turquoise strip and adhere it vertically to the left of the record.

4 Glue the recipes, reminders, and photo in place. Apply two metallic red squares over the corners of the recipes.

5 Use metallic silver to add journaling around the record and beside the photo.

Coconut Milkshake

```
2   tablespoons cream of coconut
2   tablespoons unsweetened pineapple juice
2   tablespoons sweet-and-sour drink mix
2   tablespoons half-and-half
1   tablespoons lime juice
    Crushed ice
    Pineapple wedges (optional)
    Maraschino cherries (optional)
```

In a blender container, combine cream of coconut, pineapple juice, sweet-and-sour drink mix, half-and-half, and lime juice. Add 1/2 cup crushed ice; cover and blend. Pour into two glasses. Fill glasses with additional crushed ice. If desired, garnish with a thin pineapple wedge and a cherry. Serve immediately.

Use your manners.

Thank the cook.

with your mouth closed.

The Best Burgers in the World

```
1-1/2 pounds 80-percent-lean ground beef
1     teaspoon kosher salt
1/2   teaspoon freshly ground pepper
4     super-size English muffins, split
      garlic clove, halved
1     tablespoon extra virgin olive oil
8     fresh basil leaves
4     tomato slices
```

Divide beef into quarters. Shape each piece into a 3/4-inch-thick patty.

Prepare a covered grill for direct grilling. Combine salt and pepper in a cup; sprinkle over both sides of patties. Grill patties about 15 minutes, turning every 4 minutes until an instant-read meat thermometer inserted in the side of each burger registers 160 degrees F.

While burgers are cooking, grill muffins, cut side down, for 1-1/2 to 2 minutes, until toasted. Rub garlic on toasted side, then brush each half with oil. Place basil leaves on bottom halves of muffins. Top with burgers, tomato slices and top halves of muffins.

Baked Sweet Potato Fries

```
    Nonstick cooking spray
1   pound medium sweet potatoes
1   tablespoon margarine or butter, melted
1/4 teaspoon salt
```

Lightly coat a 15x10x1-inch baking pan with cooking spray. Scrub potatoes; cut lengthwise into quarters. Cut each quarter into two wedges. Arrange potatoes in a single layer in pan. Combine margarine or butter and salt. Brush onto potatoes. Bake in a 425 degree F oven for 20 to 30 minutes or until brown and tender.

Who Says Guys Can't Cook?!

USE A BLACK-AND-WHITE WALLET-SIZE PHOTO TO BLEND WITH THE COMPOSITION.

USE A SIMPLE FONT TO PRINT RECIPES ON A COMPUTER.

LITTLE COOKIES, BIG TASTE

No matter whether we're talking cookies or cooks, the more the merrier!

CHILD'S ROLLING PIN, CIRCA 1950

WHAT YOU NEED

Recipe

Photos

12-inch square of pink, green, and white stripe paper

Card stock in pink, green, and white

Chalk in yellow and pink

¼-inch green buttons

Thread in pink and green; needle

Silver charms with cooking theme

Computer and printer

Paper cutter

Thick white crafts glue; adhesive

WHAT TO DO

1 Crop photos and mount, if desired, on pink or green card stock; trim ⅛-inch borders.

2 Print a headline, caption, recipe, and journaling on white card stock. Chalk the white paper for a softer look. Mount printed pieces on pink, green, or a stitched-together combination.

3 Tie pink thread through the buttons; knot and trim the ends. Glue to the headline corners.

4 Sew charms to small pieces of card stock and to the recipe.

5 Arrange and adhere the elements to the stripe background paper.

GLUE BUTTONS WITH KNOTTED THREAD TO THE HEADLINE CORNERS.

OMIT MATTING FOR CLOSE-UP PHOTOS.

SEW SILVER CHARMS TO CARD STOCK RECTANGLES.

STITCH THE EDGES TOGETHER FOR A TWO-TONE MOUNTING PIECE.

APPLY PINK AND YELLOW CHALK TO WHITE CARD STOCK FOR A SUBTLE APPEARANCE.

Little Cookies, Big Taste

Squeeze hard, Alex!!!!

Spritz cookies are soooo... good. We made these a lot growing up. Great-Grandma Johnson always used almond extract in hers. The day we made these we had 3 cookie presses. The old one (Diane's holding), the not so old one (Grandma's holding) & the new press (Dawn's holding).

Spritz Cookies

2¼ c. flour
½ tsp. baking powder
1 c. shortening
¾ c. sugar
1 egg - beaten
1 tsp. almond
Cream shortening, add sugar slowly & beat until light. Add egg, extract & dry ingredients. Add any color of food coloring you want. Bake @ 350 degrees.

A MOTTLED BACKGROUND ADDS TEXTURE WITHOUT OVERPOWERING THE DESIGN.

TEAR THE EDGES OF THE MOUNTING PAPER FOR INTEREST.

OUTLINE THE LETTERING WITH HAND-DRAWN DASHED LINES.

GLITTER DIE-CUT LETTERS FOR SPARKLE.

INCLUDE A PHOTO OF THE FINISHED BAKED GOODS AND THE PROUD BAKERS.

SUGARED DOUGHNUTS

Grandma's hand-me-down recipe makes delicious doughnuts and happy cooks.

WHAT YOU NEED

Recipe

Photos

12-inch square and 8½×11-inch sheet of mottled gold paper

Rust card stock

Alphabet die cuts

Gold fine glitter

Rust fine-line marking pen

Paper cutter

Computer and printer

Tape, such as Terrifically Tacky Tape

Adhesive

WHAT TO DO

1 Computer-generate journaling on smaller sheet of mottled paper. Crop journaling and photos as desired. Mount journaling, photos, and recipe on rust card stock. Tear card stock edges, leaving approximately ¼-inch borders.

2 Trace die cut letters on tape and cut out; apply to background. Sprinkle glitter on each letter. Shake off excess.

3 Outline each letter with short dashed marking pen lines. Outline journaling block with long dashed lines.

4 Adhere elements in place.

DONUT CUTTERS, CIRCA 1920 AND 1940

GOBBLE GOBBLE

Honor turkey-time treats and the baker with this quick and easy page done in autumn colors.

WHAT YOU NEED

Recipe

Photo

12-inch squares of card stock in rust, gold, and brown

12-inch square of coordinating plaid paper

Turkey sticker

Computer and printer

Corner rounder

Scissors; paper cutter; ruler

Adhesive

WHAT TO DO

1 Tear a ragged 1-inch strip from plaid paper. Adhere to gold card stock. Tear gold card stock approximately ½ inch from edge of plaid paper. Adhere the layered papers to the edge of the rust card stock.

2 Trim photo as desired, using a corner rounder. Mount on brown card stock and trim ⅛ inch beyond the edge of the photo.

3 Cut a 3¼-inch square from gold card stock. Mount on brown and trim ⅛ inch beyond the edge of the gold. Place a turkey sticker in the center.

4 Round the corners of the recipe. Mount the recipe on brown paper. Trim ⅛ inch beyond the edge of the recipe.

5 Use a computer to generate the letter patterns for the headline. Print on brown and cut out each letter. Cut two 1½×2-inch rectangles from plaid paper.

6 Adhere the elements to the background, placing a plaid paper rectangle behind each G.

USE A COMPUTER TO MAKE PATTERNS FOR HEADLINE LETTERING.

MOUNT A STICKER ON LAYERED PAPERS FOR AN ARTISTIC ELEMENT.

ANCHOR THE HEADLINE WITH PLAID PAPER RECTANGLES.

TEAR PAPER STRIPS FOR A RAGGED COLOR BAR AT THE EDGE OF THE PAGE.

ROUND THE CORNERS OF THE RECIPE AND CUT THE MOUNTING PAPER CORNERS STRAIGHT.

PUMPKIN BARS

APPLE BOWL, CIRCA 1940

As you sift through family papers, collect all the recipes you find, even if they're written on the backs of envelopes.

Bailey picks some pumpkins at an Ankeny patch, Oct. '94, age 1

PHOTOCOPY A HANDWRITTEN RECIPE ON CREAM CARD STOCK.

TURN PAPER SQUARES ON POINT.

USE CHALK TO ADD AN AGED EFFECT TO SOLID PAPER.

CHOOSE STICKERS THAT REFLECT THE THEME.

WRITE JOURNALING NEATLY IN WHITE SPACE.

BALANCE THE COMPOSITION WITH SIMPLE PAPER STRIPS.

WHAT YOU NEED

Recipe; photo
8½×11-inch sheets of card stock
  in white, dark orange, cream,
  olive green, and beige
Brown chalk; paper cutter
Kitchen-theme stickers
2 small dark orange brads; ruler
Brown marking pen
Adhesive

WHAT TO DO

1 Crop the photo and mount on dark orange; trim narrow borders.

2 Photocopy a handwritten recipe on cream card stock; trim. Mount on beige and trim.

3 Print the recipe title on beige. Insert two brads at the end of the title; trim. Draw a brown broken line around the edges.

4 Cut a ⅝×11-inch strip from green. Cut two 1½-inch squares from dark orange and three from beige. Chalk the edges of the beige squares; press a sticker in each center. Adhere squares to strip, leaving ½ inch at the top and

bottom and centering the remaining square. Layer the orange squares on point on the back of the strip. Adhere strip to left edge of background paper.

5 Cut a ½-wide strip the width of mounted recipe.

6 Using the photo as a guide, adhere the elements in place.

7 Add journaling in brown marking pen.

BRIDGEPORT CHILI

Sometimes where one lives triggers memories of special recipes, such as this chili recipe from Bridgeport, Illinois.

WHAT YOU NEED

Recipe; photo
8½×11-inch card stock
  in white, green, cream, and
  light gray and scrap of white
Kitchen-theme stickers
Paper cutter; ruler
Green fine-line marking pen
Pen with disappearing ink
Computer and printer; adhesive

WHAT TO DO

1 Trim the photo and mount on gray; trim. Mount on green; trim.

2 Cut a ½×4-inch strip from cream. Cut a ⅛×4-inch strip from green. Center and adhere the green strip to the cream strip.

Adhere horizontally to left side of page, ⅛ inch from the top.

3 Photocopy a handwritten recipe on cream card stock; trim. Layer and mount on gray, cream, and green, trimming each border approximately ⅛ inch wide.

4 Print the recipe title in a small font on cream card stock. Apply a sticker below the title; trim. Mount on green; trim.

5 Using the photo as a guide, adhere elements in place.

6 Add journaling in green marking pen.

CUT PAPER STRIPS FOR INTERESTING DETAIL.

Bridgeport Chili

Chicago from Sears Tower, 1986

CHOOSE STICKERS THAT CARRY OUT THE THEME.

FOR NEAT JOURNALING, DRAW GUIDE LINES USING A PEN WITH DISAPPEARING INK.

TO HIGHLIGHT RECIPE, MOUNT ON SEVERAL PAPERS.

BRIDGEPORT CHILI
1 CAN BROOKS "CHILI HOT BEANS" 22 OZ
½ lb. Hbgr
⅓ can H₂O
Hottest Sauce Available 2 TBSP.
chili powder
(garlic salt)
makes CHILI for 2-3

My husband, Jay, spent four years at the Illinois College of Optometry in Chicago, graduating in 1987. While there he lived with fellow students in a modest apartment in Bridgeport on Chicago's south side. Jay occasionally took to the kitchen, perfecting his recipe for chili, written here on the back of an IED form. To save time, he would cook the chili and eat it right out of the pan, which mortified me. We still use this recipe today.

REINFORCE THE THEME OF
A RECIPE WITH FOOD-RELATED
DIE-CUT LETTERING.

TURN CONTRASTING
SQUARES ON POINT.

TEAR MOUNTING PAPER EDGES
FOR A RAGGED LOOK.

USE SILHOUETTE STICKERS TO ADD
SHAPES IN OPEN SPACES.

USE A PLAYFUL FONT TO GENERATE TYPE.

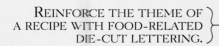

COOKIES

*Kids of all ages love cookies and milk
and here's one grand way to show it!*

WHAT YOU NEED

Recipe

Photos

*Three 12-inch squares of bright
    blue card stock*

12-inch square of red card stock

Scrap of white card stock

*Chocolate chip lettering, such as
    PhotoGenix*

Black alphabet stickers

*Stickers with cookies and milk
    themes*

Paper cutter; ruler

Computer and printer

Adhesive

WHAT TO DO

1 Crop the photos and
mount on red paper;
trim ¼-inch borders beyond
the edges.

2 Computer-generate the
cookie recipe and
journaling. Print on bright
blue paper. Print the recipe
on white.

3 Tear a 2¼-inch strip from
the edge of one sheet of
blue card stock. Mount on red,
leaving a ⅛-inch space at the
straight edge. Tear red
approximately ¼ inch from the

edge of the blue. Mount to the
top of one background sheet.

4 Mount journaling on red;
tear away borders.

5 Mount recipe on a 4-inch
red paper square set on
point. Tear a ¾×4-inch strip
and adhere over milk recipe.

6 Adhere elements in place,
including food stickers
and headline.

THE PERFECT APPLE

Once the photos are cropped and mounted, you can put these pages together in a jiffy.

WHAT YOU NEED

Recipe

Photos

Two 12-inch squares of card stock in medium green

Card stock in light yellow and light green

Watercolor-print paper in green and yellow

Apple-theme die cuts

Computer and printer

Date stamp

Paper cutter; ruler

Adhesive

WHAT TO DO

1 Crop the photos and mount on yellow paper; trim ⅛ inch beyond photo. Mount on light green if desired; trim a ¼-inch green border.

2 Computer-generate split headlines, journaling, and recipe, and print them on watercolor paper. Stamp a date on the journaling block and crop as desired. Layer and mount the journaling block on yellow paper and green if desired. Trim ⅛ to ¼ inch beyond yellow, cropping off the top and bottom at the yellow edge.

BALANCE PHOTOS AND COPY BLOCKS WITH DIE CUTS.

COMPUTER-GENERATE THE HEADLINE, JOURNALING, AND RECIPE FOR CONSISTENCY.

you have to pick the perfect apple..

LINE UP DIE CUTS AS A UNIT.

APPLE SLICER AND APPLE CORER, CIRCA 1950

3 Arrange photos, printed blocks, and die cuts on pages, using the pages, *below,* as a guide. For organization, notice how the components are aligned along the outer edges of the background. Adhere the elements in place.

Black's Apple Orchard is the perfect place to pick apples. We had so much fun taking the hayrack ride out to the orchard to pick the hugest, tastiest apples. The apple in Amanda's hand was the largest apple any of us had ever seen.

SEP   2002

To make the perfect caramel apple!

Caramel Apples

1   T butter
1   cups brown sugar
6 T water
popsicle sticks
8 - 10 apples

Melt butter in saucepan. Add brown sugar and water. Stir until smooth. Gently bring to a boil, cover and simmer for 3 minutes. Remove from heat. Dip apples and place on greased cookie sheet. Chill for 1 hour.

{ KEEP SPACE BETWEEN ELEMENTS CONSISTENT.

{ USE A STAMP TO DATE THE JOURNALING BLOCK.

{ A SOFT WATERCOLOR PAPER COORDINATES WITH SOLID PAPERS.

HOT MULLED CIDER

For a pretty page sans photos, this design is dedicated to a favorite cider recipe and uses coordinating papers, slide mounts, charms, and die cuts.

WHAT YOU NEED

Recipe

12-inch squares of card stock in black and textured black and scraps of red; white paper

12-inch square of red and black plaid paper

Black slide mounts, such as Jest Charming

Snowflake charms, such as Making Memories

Dimensional mug die cuts

Computer and printer

Scissors; ruler; paper cutter

Adhesive

WHAT TO DO

1 Trim plaid paper to measure 11½ inches square. Center and adhere to the black card stock.

2 Cut a 12×3¾-inch strip from black textured card stock. Adhere horizontally 3¼ inches from the bottom of the page.

3 Cut a 2½×6½-inch rectangle from red card stock. Mount on black; trim a ⅛-inch border. Adhere three slide mounts on the red rectangle.

4 Cut a 2½-inch square of red card stock. Adhere a slide mount in the center.

5 Print headline on white paper. Use as patterns to cut lettering from black. Adhere three slide mounts diagonally for headline. Adhere lettering in place.

6 Adhere the recipe and papers with slide mounts to the background. Embellish with snowflake charms and mug die cuts.

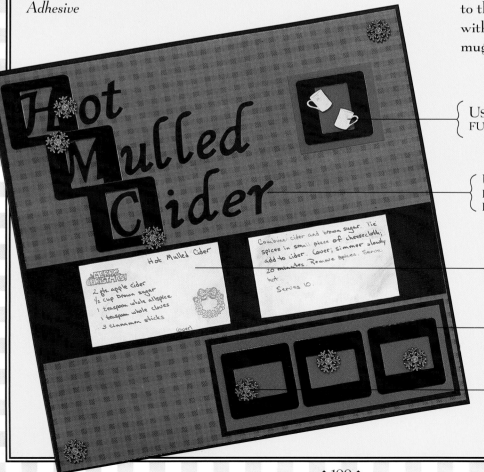

USE DIE CUTS FOR A FUN EMBELLISHMENT.

USE A COMPUTER TO MAKE PATTERNS FOR HEADLINE LETTERING.

PHOTOCOPY BOTH SIDES OF A TWO-SIDED RECIPE.

USE SLIDE MOUNTS AS GRAPHIC FRAME ELEMENTS.

ARRANGE SNOWFLAKE CHARMS IN CORNERS, ON SLIDE MOUNTS, AND ON HEADLINE.

CREAM-FILLED CUPCAKES

When your little munchkin helps make cupcakes, this page design is as sweet as frosting.

CHOOSE LETTERS THAT CARRY OUT A THEME.

USE FLANNEL PAPER FOR SOFT TEXTURE.

USE A CIRCLE CUTTER FOR PERFECT CROPS.

TEAR CARD STOCK TO CREATE IRREGULAR EDGES.

COORDINATE THE PAPER COLORS WITH THE LETTERING.

WHAT YOU NEED

Recipes

Photos

12-inch squares of card stock in white and brown and scraps of white

12-inch square of white flannel paper

Cupcake sticker letters

Circle cutter

Paper cutter; ruler

Adhesive

WHAT TO DO

1 Cut a 6×12-inch rectangle from flannel paper. Adhere to the left side of the white card stock. Cut a 12×7-inch rectangle from brown paper. Tear one long edge. Tear the piece in half lengthwise. Overlap the two pieces slightly and adhere to the right edge of the white card stock.

2 Use cupcake letters to spell out the headline vertically and horizontally. Adhere in place.

3 Crop the photos, using a circle cutter if desired. Mount the photos on white or brown card stock. Trim ⅛- to ¼-inch borders around photos, using the circle cutter for the round photos.

4 Mount one recipe on brown and trim ⅛ inch from the recipe edge. Adhere the recipes and photos in place.

CUPCAKE POKES, CIRCA 1960

HOT WINGS

Mini mosaic tiles add dimension to this now-funny story of how a near cooking catastrophe helped rename a recipe.

WHAT YOU NEED

Recipe; photos

Two 12-inch squares each of card stock in red and black; vellum

3/8-inch mosaic crafts tiles in yellow, orange, and red

Computer and printer; paper cutter; adhesive foam mounts, such as Pop Dots; adhesive

WHAT TO DO

1 Tear 3- and 5-inch-wide strips from black card stock, leaving one straight edge on each piece. Adhere the strips horizontally on the red card stock, 3-inch strips at the top and the 5-inch strips at the bottom.

2 Crop the photos.

3 Computer-generate headlines, journaling, and recipe; print on vellum.

4 Arrange photos, printed blocks, and headline on pages. Adhere in place. Adhere tiles in place using mounts.

USE CLOSE-UP SHOTS TO HELP TELL THE STORY.

PRINT TYPE ON VELLUM TO ALLOW THE BACKGROUND TO SOFTLY SHOW THROUGH.

BACK THE HEADLINE WITH A PHOTO OF THE FOOD.

USE ADHESIVE FOAM MOUNTS TO ADHERE MOSAIC TILES IN PLACE.

LAYER AND MOUNT TORN BLACK PAPER STRIPS TO RED CARD STOCK.

Flamin' Jeff's Hot Wings

ADD A CONTRASTING PAPER STRIP
AT EACH END OF HEADLINE.

ADD DIMENSIONAL
STICKERS TO FILL PAGE.

CUT PAPER STRIPS TO FRAME
COPY BLOCKS.

USE FOAM MOUNTS TO RAISE THE DIE
CUTS FROM THE BACKGROUND.

OMIT THE DATE FROM JOURNALING WHEN
THE PHOTO HAS A RECORDED DATE.

The Kids and I gave Kim a Grill for his Birthday and he couldn't wait to try out all his favorite grilling recipies

Barbecue Sauce
1/2 cup catsup
1/4 cup vinegar
1/4 cup water
1 small onion
1 1/2 teaspoons packed brown sugar
1 1/2 teaspoons prepared mustard
1 1/2 teaspoons Worcestershire sauce
1/4 teaspoons salt
1/8 teaspoon pepper
Mix all ingredients.

Spicy Potato Salad
2 pounds of red potatoes
1/4 cup chopped green onions
1/2 cup sour cream
1 teaspoon salt
1/8 teaspoon salt
1 cup mayonnaise
1/4 cup jalapenos'
1/4 cup chopped sweet pickles
2 hard cooked eggs

BBQ Sauce

CHILLIN' AND GRILLIN'

If you know someone who loves to cook barbecue-style, here's a great way to remember savory at-the-grill recipes.

WHAT YOU NEED

Recipes
Photos
Two 12-inch sheets of black fleck
  card stock
Card stock in light yellow and red
Dimensional barbecue
  die-cut stickers
Computer and printer
Paper cutter
Adhesive foam mounts, such as
  Pop Dots
Adhesive

WHAT TO DO

1 Crop the photos and mount on red or yellow card stock. Cut a 3½×11-inch rectangle of light yellow card stock.

2 Print the headline, journaling, and recipes on yellow card stock. Trim around the type; mount the journaling on red. Trim ⅛ inch beyond the yellow. To frame the recipes, cut ¼-inch-wide strips from red.

3 Adhere photos and add frame strips in place on background card stock. Trim frame strips at edges of background paper if necessary.

4 Use foam mounts to adhere die-cut stickers the on yellow card stock strip and background.

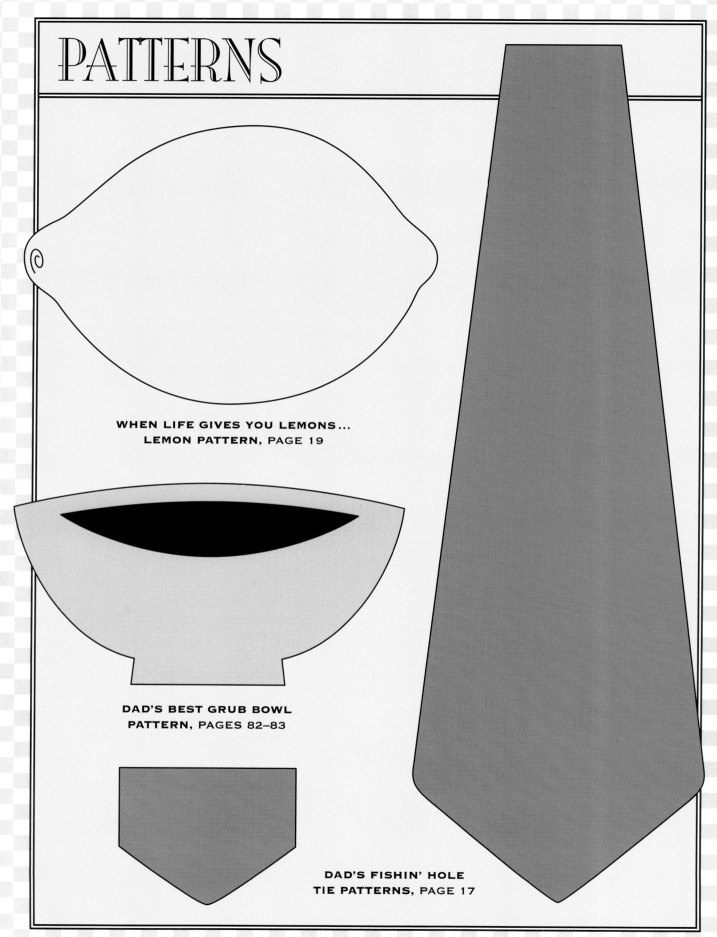

PATTERNS

WHEN LIFE GIVES YOU LEMONS…
LEMON PATTERN, PAGE 19

DAD'S BEST GRUB BOWL
PATTERN, PAGES 82–83

DAD'S FISHIN' HOLE
TIE PATTERNS, PAGE 17

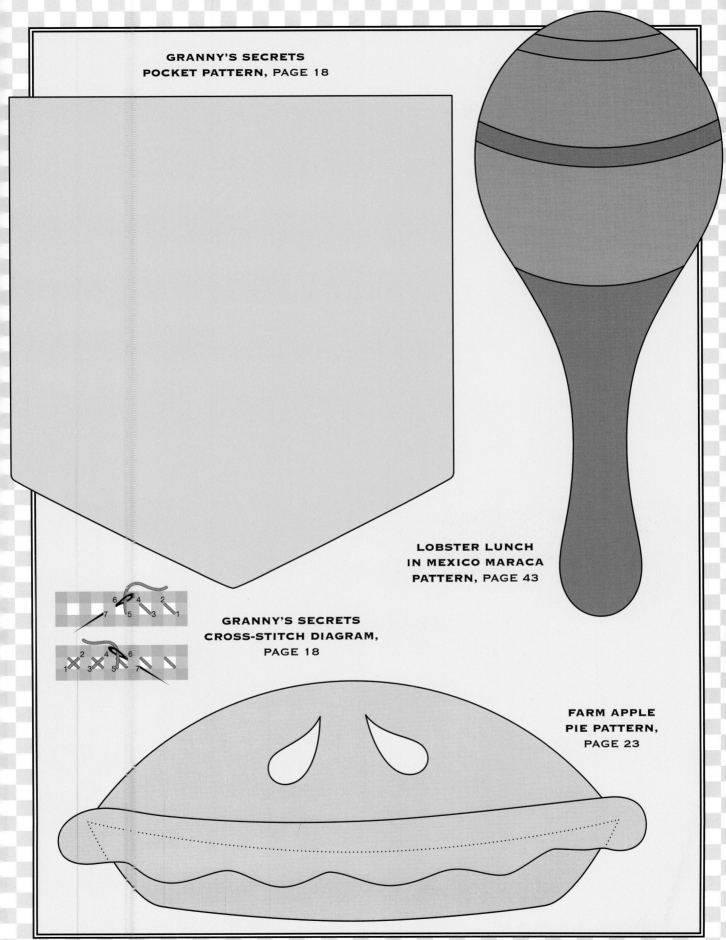

**GRANNY'S SECRETS
POCKET PATTERN, PAGE 18**

**LOBSTER LUNCH
IN MEXICO MARACA
PATTERN, PAGE 43**

**GRANNY'S SECRETS
CROSS-STITCH DIAGRAM,
PAGE 18**

**FARM APPLE
PIE PATTERN,
PAGE 23**

PATTERNS continued

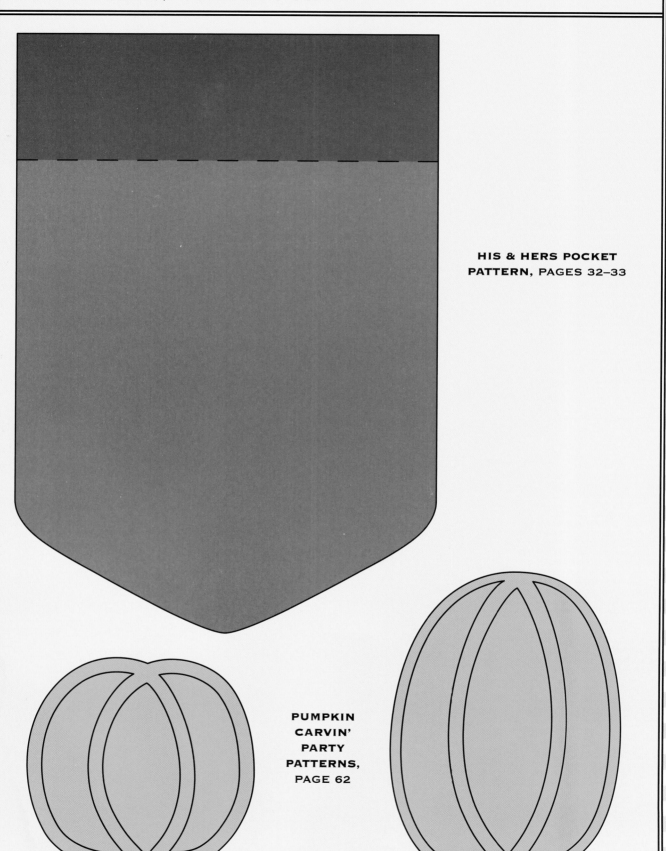

HIS & HERS POCKET
PATTERN, PAGES 32–33

PUMPKIN
CARVIN'
PARTY
PATTERNS,
PAGE 62

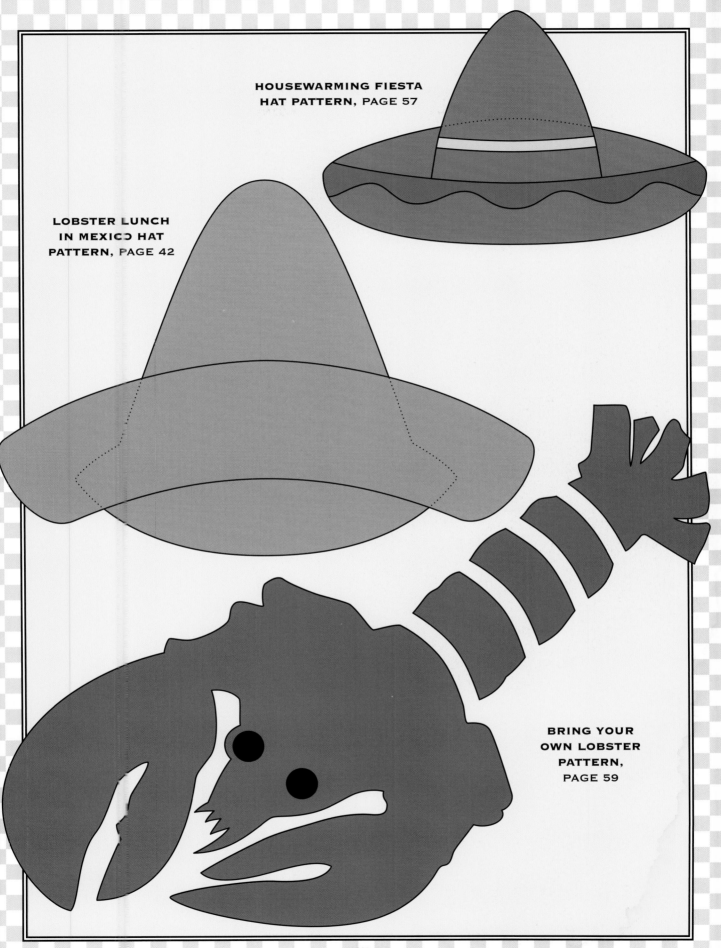

HOUSEWARMING FIESTA
HAT PATTERN, PAGE 57

LOBSTER LUNCH
IN MEXICO HAT
PATTERN, PAGE 42

BRING YOUR
OWN LOBSTER
PATTERN,
PAGE 59

PATTERNS continued

**SUPER BOWL
GOALPOST PATTERNS,
PAGE 60**

**SUPER BOWL
FOOTBALL PATTERN,
PAGE 60**

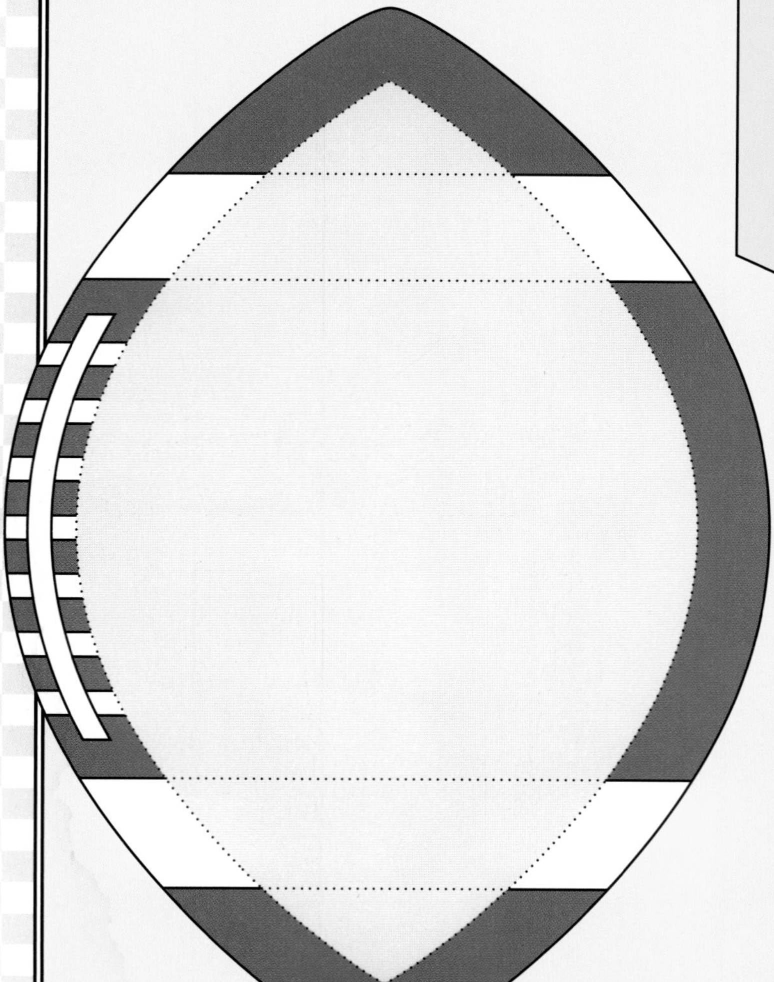

DAD'S BEST GRUB
COOK PATTERNS,
PAGES 82–83

SOURCES & CREDITS

ADHESIVES
Aleenes
duncancrafts.com

Centis
Centis Consumer Products
Division
888/236-8476

Elmer's Glue Stick
800/848-9400
elmers.com
comments@elmers.com

Suze Weinberg Design
Studio
732/761-2400
732/761-2410 (fax)
Suzenj@aol.com

Tombow USA
800/835-3232
tombowusa.com

BRADS
Magic Scraps
972/238-1838
magicscraps.com

BUTTONS
Le Bouton Buttons
Blumenthal Lansing Co.
563/538-4211
563/538-4243 (fax)
sales@buttonsplus.com

DIE CUTS
Cock a Doodle
800/262-9727
cockadoodle.com

Deluxe Cuts
480/497-9005
707/922-2175 (fax)
deluxecuts.com

Fresh Cuts
Rebecca Sower
EK Success Ltd.
eksuccess.com

Griff's Shortcuts
989/894-5916
griffs-shortcuts.com

Little Extras
361/814-9191
littleextrasdiecuts.com

Stamping Station
801/444-3838
stampingstation.com

EYELETS
Persnippity
801/523-3338
persnippity.com

FIBERS
Cut-It-Up
530/389-2233
cut-it-up.com

FOAM SQUARES
Therm O Web
800/323-0799

**OPAQUE WRITERS &
WATERPROOF
MARKERS**
EK Success Ltd.
eksuccess.com
(Wholesale only. Available
at most crafts stores.)

PRESS-ON GEMS
Stampa Rosa, Inc.
707/527-8267
stamparosa.com

**RUBBER STAMPS &
INK PADS**
Art Impressions
800/393-2014
artimpressions.com

Stampin' Up!
801/601-5400
stampinup.com

**RUB-ON LETTERING
& MOTIFS**
Chartpak, Inc.
800/628-1910
800/762-7918 (fax)
chartpak.com

The Paper Patch
www.paperpatch.com
(Wholesale only. Available
at most crafts stores.)

Scrapbook Borders
scrapbookborders.com

**SCISSORS, PUNCHES,
& ROUNDERS**
Creative Memories
800/341-5275
creativememories.com

EK Success Ltd.
eksuccess.com
(Wholesale only. Available
at most crafts stores.)

Emagination Crafts, Inc.
866/238-9770
service@emaginationcraftsin
c.com

Fiskars Scissors
608/259-1649
fiskars.com

SCRAPBOOK PAPERS
All My Memories
888/553-1998

Anna Griffin
404/817-8170)
404/817-0590 (fax)
annagriffin.com

Art Accents
360/733-8989
artaccents.net

Bazzill Basics Paper
480/558-8557
bazzillbasics.com

Colorbök
800/366-4660
colorbok.com

Daisy D's Paper Co.
801/447-8955
daisydspaper.com

DMD, Inc.
800/805-9890

Doodlebug
801/966-9952

Family Archives
888/622-6556
heritagescrapbooks.com

Frances Meyer, Inc.
800/372-6237
francesmeyer.com

Hot Off the Press, Inc.
800/227-9595
paperpizazz.com

Karen Foster Design, Inc.
karenfosterdesign.com

Making Memories
800/286-5263
makingmemories.com

Memories Forever
Westrim Crafts
800/727-2727
westrimcrafts.com

The Paper Loft
866/254-1961 (toll free)
paperloft.com
(Wholesale only. Available
at most crafts stores.)

Pixie Press
888/834-2883
pixiepress.com

Plaid Enterprises, Inc.
800/842-4197
plaidonline.com

Provo Craft
provocraft.com
(Wholesale only. Available
at most crafts stores.)

CANNING JARS, CIRCA 1950

INDEX

Sandylion
800/387-4215
905/475-0523
(International)
sandylion.com

Scrap-ease What's New, Ltd.
800/272-3874
480/832-2928 (fax)
whatsnewltd.com

Sweetwater
14711 Road 15
Fort Morgan, CO 80701
970/867-4428

Two Busy Moms
800/272-4794
TwoBusyMoms.com

Westrim Crafts
800/727-2727

Wübie Prints
wubieprints.com
(Wholesale only. Available
at most crafts stores.)

STICKERS
Canson
800/628-9283
canson-us.com

The Gifted Line
John Grossman, Inc.
310/390-9900

Highsmith
800/558-3899
highsmith.com

K & Co.
816/389-4150
KandCompany.com

me & my BIG ideas
949/589-4607
meandmybigideas.com

Mrs. Grossmans Paper Co.
800/429-4549
mrsgrossmans.com

Once Upon a Scribble
702/896-2181
onceuponascribble.com

Paper House Productions
800/255-7316
paperhouseproductions.com

Paper Punch
800/397-2737

SRM Press
800/323-9589
srmpress.com
(Wholesale only. Available
at most crafts stores.)

Stickopotamus
P.O. Box 1047
Clifton, NJ 07014-1047
973/594-0540 (fax)
stickopotamus.com

DESIGNERS
Susan M. Banker—
  Pages 18–19, 30–33, 38–39,
  82–83, and 86–91.
Carol Field Dahlstrom—
  Pages 20–21.
Kelli Gould—Page 78.
Dawn Johnson—Pages
  48–49, 81, 94, and 98–101.
Tammy Kempf—Pages 14–15,
  97, and 103.
Janet Petersma—Pages 12–13,
  24–29, 66–77, and 95–96.
Diane Reams—Pages 10–11,
  22–23, 80, and 92–93.
Gayle Schadendorf—Pages
  42–43, 54, and 58–59.
Cheri Thieleke—Page 102.
Alice Wetzel—Page 85.
Sharon Widdop—Pages
  16–17, 34–35, 40–41, 44–47,
  50–53, 55–57, 60–63, and 84.
Wendy Wyckoff—Page 79.

SPECIAL THANKS TO
Donna Chesnut, Elizabeth
Dahlstrom, and Ardith
Field for sharing their
kitchen collectibles.

Index continued on page 112

INDEX continued